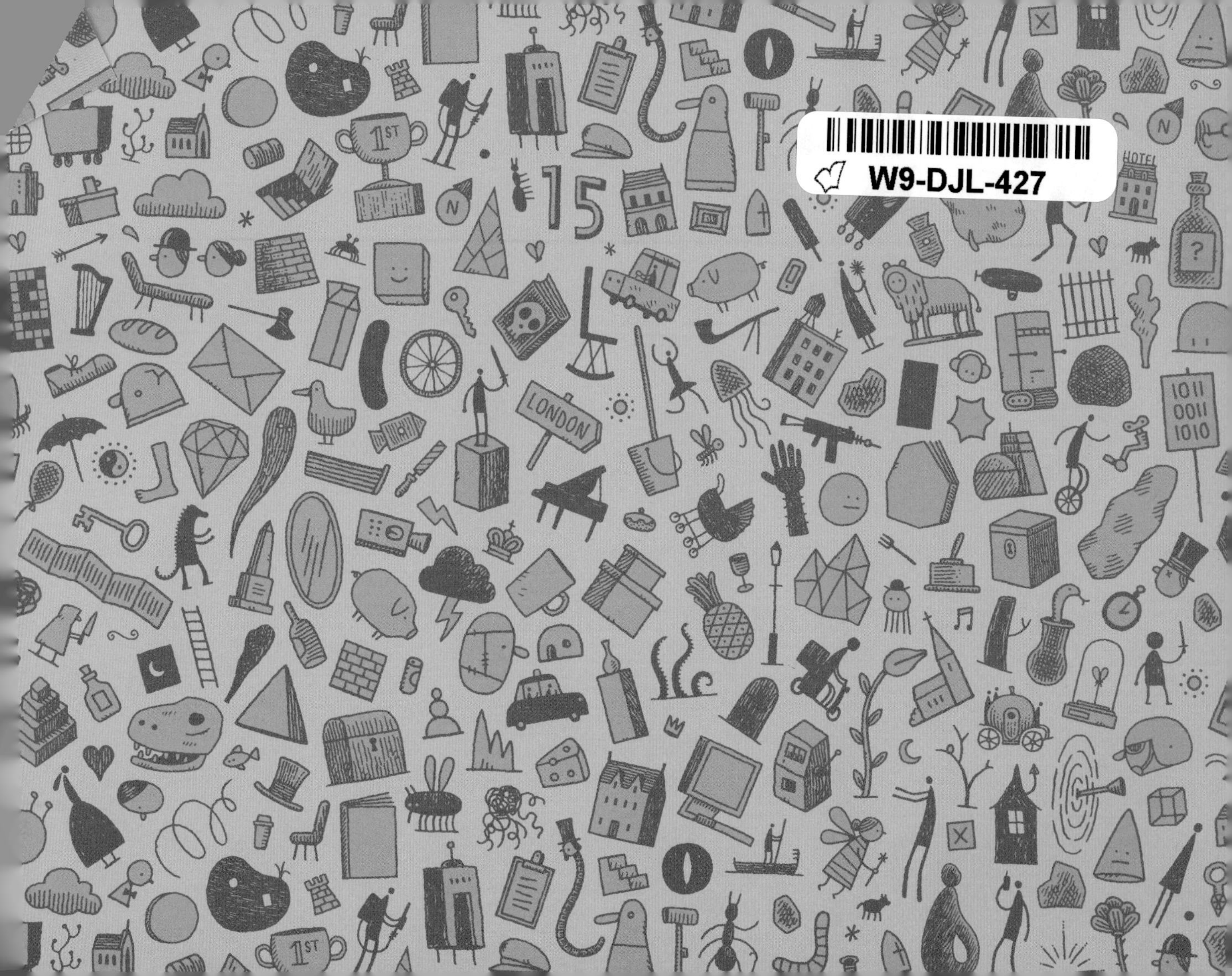
1ST
15
HOTEL
LONDON
1011
0011
1010

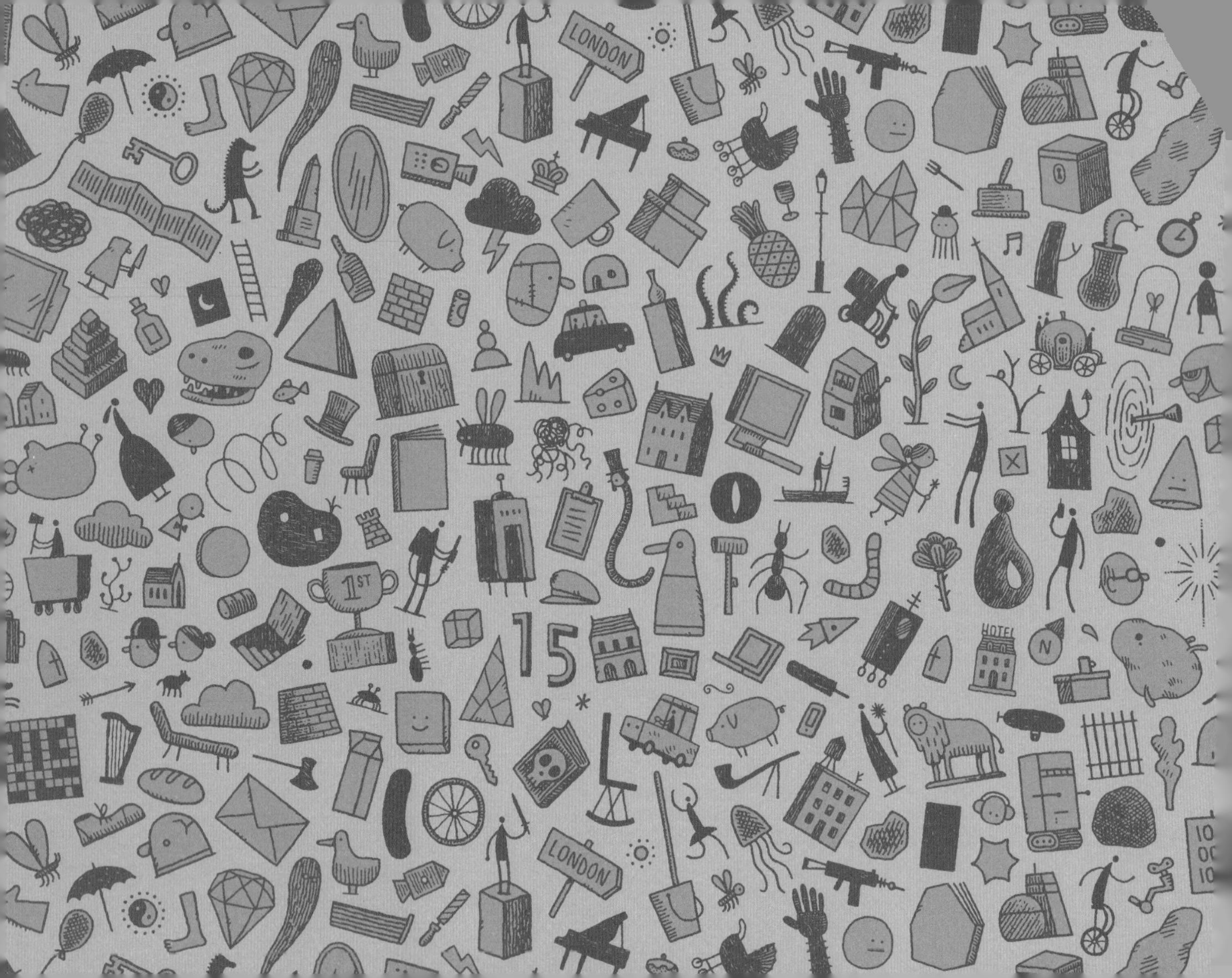
LONDON
1ST
15
HOTEL
N
LONDON

SHORT STORY
WILL YOU PUBLISH MY SHORT STORIES?
NO.
THE END

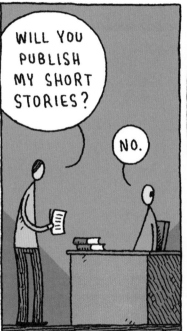

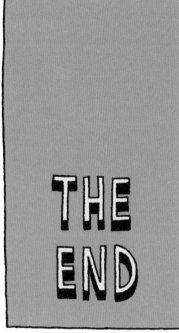

FIRST HARDCOVER EDITION: MARCH 2013
PRINTED IN CHINA
10 9 8 7 6 5 4 3 2 1

LIBRARY AND ARCHIVES CANADA
CATALOGUING IN PUBLICATION

GAULD, TOM
YOU'RE ALL JUST JEALOUS OF MY JETPACK / TOM GAULD

ISBN 978-1-77046-104-8

I. GRAPHIC NOVELS.   I. TITLE
PN6737.G38 Y682 2013   741.5'9411   C2012-905367-8

PUBLISHED IN THE USA BY:
DRAWN & QUARTERLY
A CLIENT PUBLISHER OF
FARRAR, STRAUS AND GIROUX
18 WEST 18TH STREET
NEW YORK, NY 10011
ORDERS: 888.330.8477

PUBLISHED IN CANADA BY:
DRAWN & QUARTERLY
A CLIENT PUBLISHER OF
RAINCOAST BOOKS
2440 VIKING WAY
RICHMOND, BC V6V 1N2
ORDERS: 800.663.5714

DISTRIBUTED IN THE
UNITED KINGDOM BY:
PUBLISHERS GROUP UK
63-66 HATTON GARDEN
LONDON
EC1N 8LE
INFO@PGUK.CO.UK

YOU'RE ALL JUST JEALOUS OF MY JETPACK

COMICS BY
TOM GAULD

DRAWN & QUARTERLY

FOR DAPHNE AND IRIS

THE MOUSE, THE BIRD AND THE DIFFICULT NOVEL

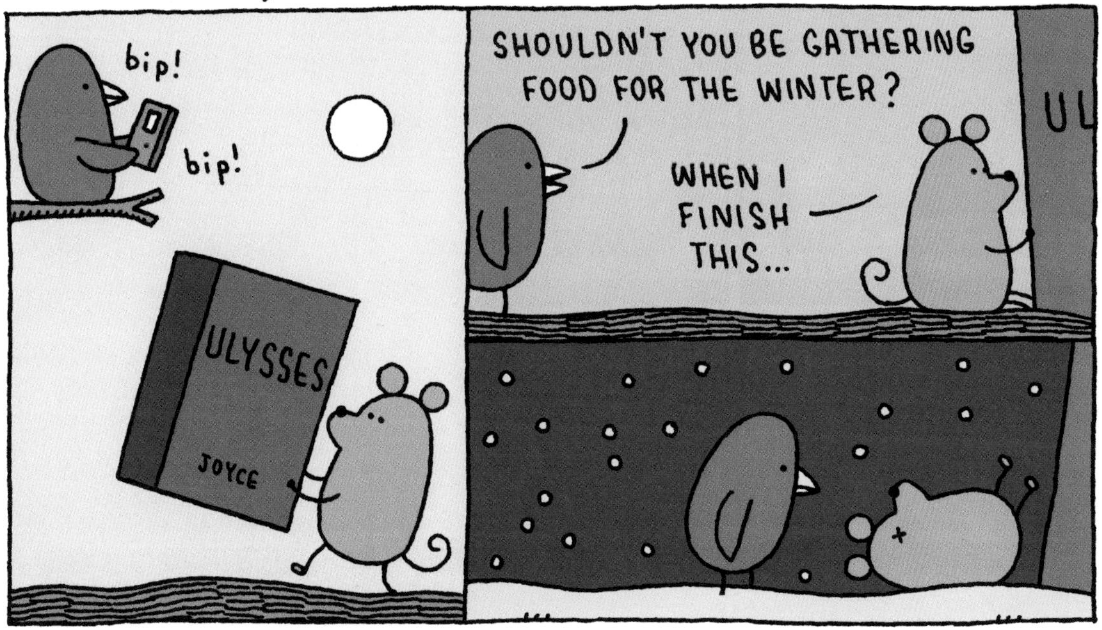
bip!
bip!
ULYSSES
JOYCE
SHOULDN'T YOU BE GATHERING FOOD FOR THE WINTER?
WHEN I FINISH THIS...
UL

NIGHT IN THE CONSULTING ROOM

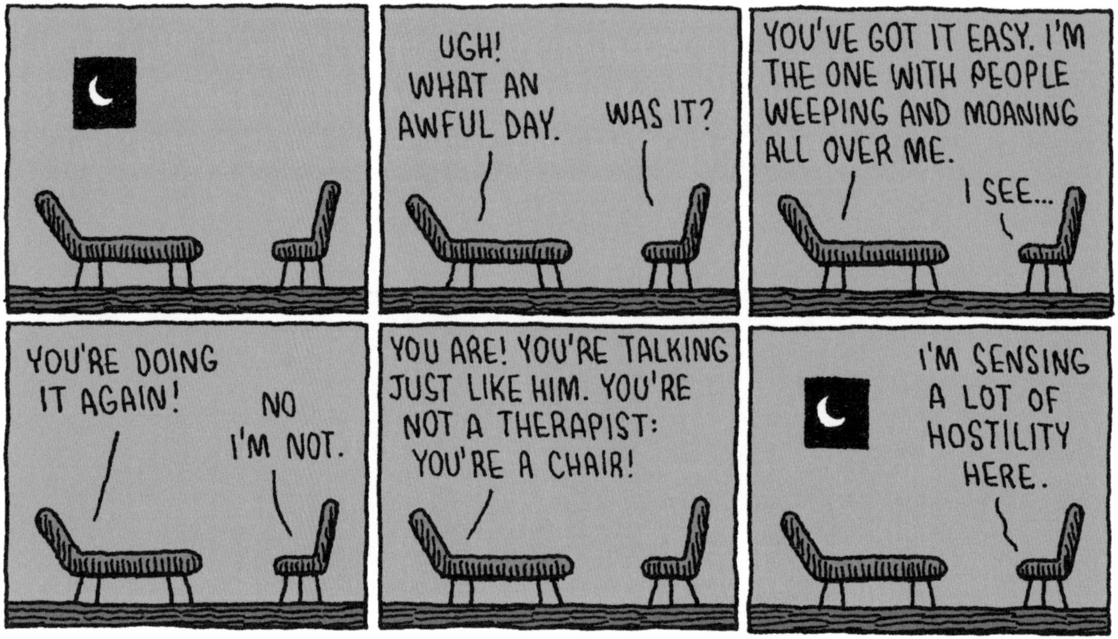
UGH! WHAT AN AWFUL DAY.
WAS IT?
YOU'VE GOT IT EASY. I'M THE ONE WITH PEOPLE WEEPING AND MOANING ALL OVER ME.
I SEE...
YOU'RE DOING IT AGAIN!
NO I'M NOT.
YOU ARE! YOU'RE TALKING JUST LIKE HIM. YOU'RE NOT A THERAPIST: YOU'RE A CHAIR!
I'M SENSING A LOT OF HOSTILITY HERE.

1592, WILLIAM SHAKESPEARE ADDRESSES HIS CAST

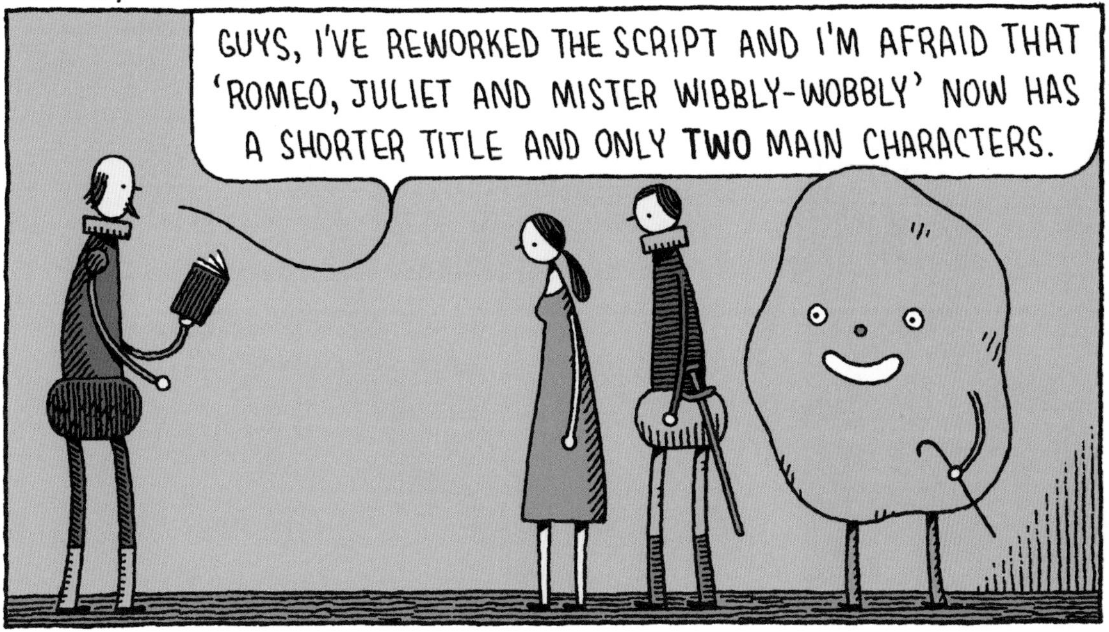
GUYS, I'VE REWORKED THE SCRIPT AND I'M AFRAID THAT 'ROMEO, JULIET AND MISTER WIBBLY-WOBBLY' NOW HAS A SHORTER TITLE AND ONLY TWO MAIN CHARACTERS.

CONTROLS FOR 'RHETT BUTLER: THE VIDEOGAME'
SCANDALIZE
CAUSTIC REMARK
CHARM
PROPOSAL OF MARRIAGE
DRUNKEN THREAT
INVITATION TO DANCE
DUEL
BOURBON

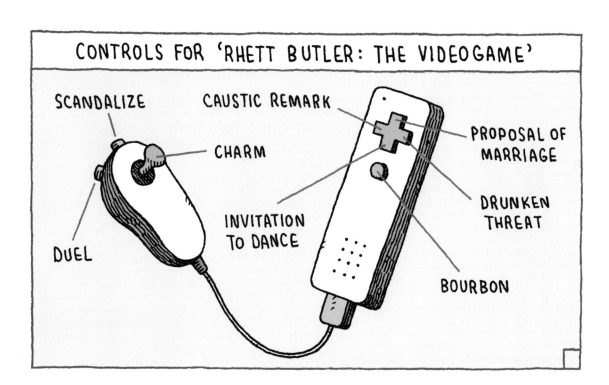

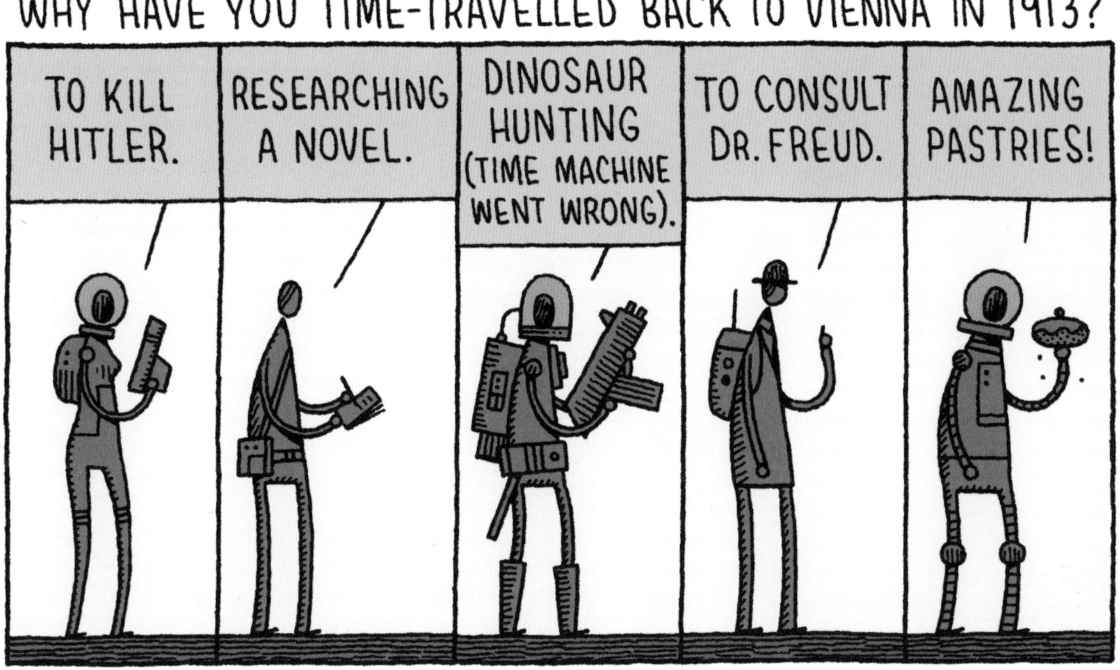
WHY HAVE YOU TIME-TRAVELLED BACK TO VIENNA IN 1913?
TO KILL HITLER.
RESEARCHING A NOVEL.
DINOSAUR HUNTING (TIME MACHINE WENT WRONG).
TO CONSULT DR. FREUD.
AMAZING PASTRIES!

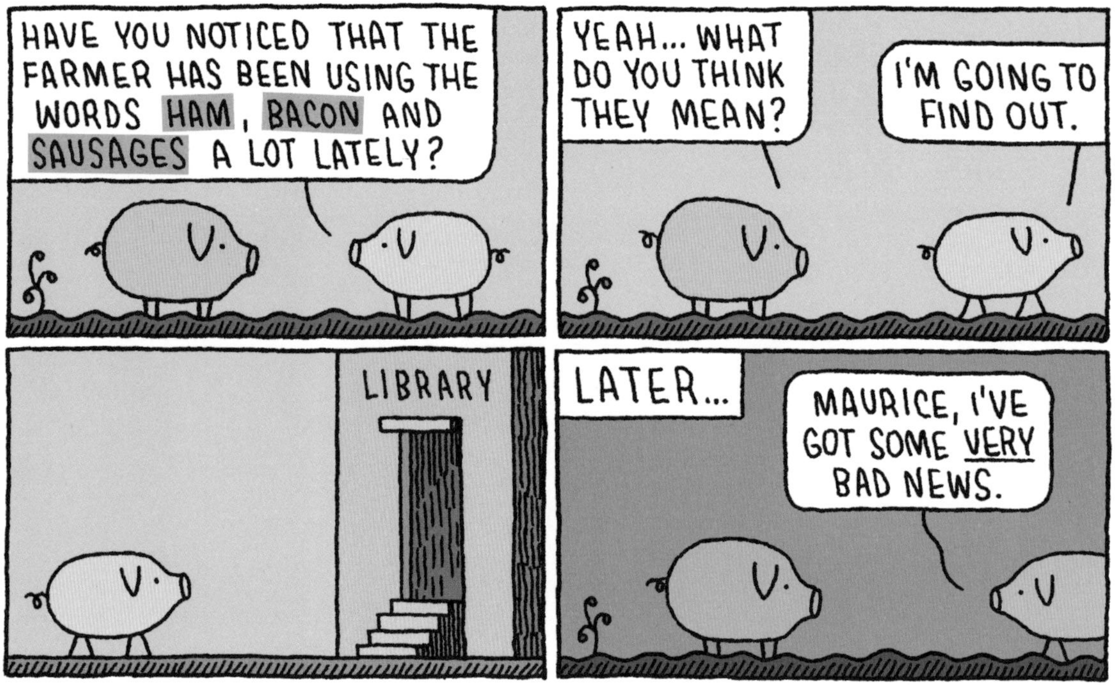
HAVE YOU NOTICED THAT THE FARMER HAS BEEN USING THE WORDS HAM, BACON AND SAUSAGES A LOT LATELY?
YEAH... WHAT DO YOU THINK THEY MEAN?
I'M GOING TO FIND OUT.
LIBRARY
LATER...
MAURICE, I'VE GOT SOME VERY BAD NEWS.

INSTITUTE OF NEOLOGISMS.

DEPARTMENT OF EVERYDAY LANGUAGE.

SOCIETY FOR THE PRESERVATION OF ANTIQUATED TERMINOLOGY.

CEMETERY OF FORGOTTEN WORDS.

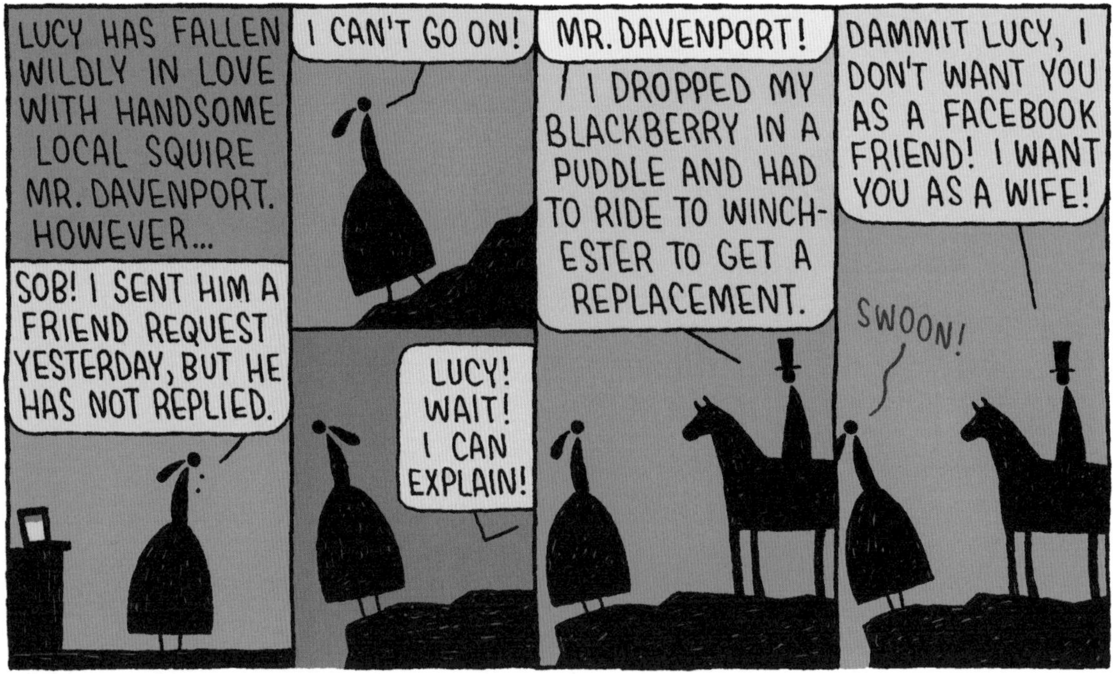
LUCY HAS FALLEN WILDLY IN LOVE WITH HANDSOME LOCAL SQUIRE MR. DAVENPORT. HOWEVER...
SOB! I SENT HIM A FRIEND REQUEST YESTERDAY, BUT HE HAS NOT REPLIED.
I CAN'T GO ON!
LUCY! WAIT! I CAN EXPLAIN!
MR. DAVENPORT!
I DROPPED MY BLACKBERRY IN A PUDDLE AND HAD TO RIDE TO WINCH-ESTER TO GET A REPLACEMENT.
DAMMIT LUCY, I DON'T WANT YOU AS A FACEBOOK FRIEND! I WANT YOU AS A WIFE!
SWOON!

THE STREET TOM WAITS GREW UP ON

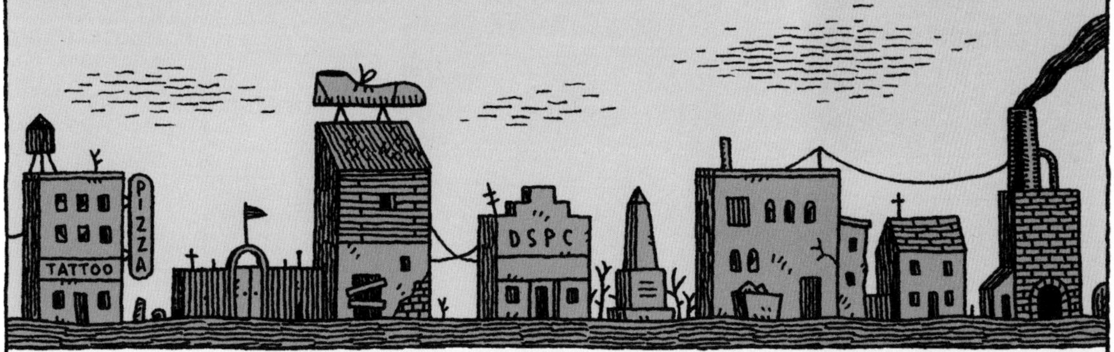
PIZZA
TATTOO
DSPC

(L-R) VERN'S ALL-NITE PIZZA 'N' TATTOO, ACCORDION PLAYERS' GRAVEYARD, ABANDONED CLOWN-SHOE FACTORY, DIVORCED SALESMEN'S POLKA CLUB, TOMB OF THE UNKNOWN CABBIE, BOOTLEG ICE-CREAM WAREHOUSE, SAINT FRANK'S HOBO ORPHANAGE, ILLEGAL UMBRELLA INCINERATOR.

FRAGMENTS OF DICKENS'S LOST NOVEL "A MEGALOSAUR'S PROGRESS"

ABANDONED AS AN EGG
A CRUEL ORPHANAGE
AN UNEXPECTED INHERITANCE
A WATCHFUL STRANGER
BECOMES A GENTLEMAN
LONDON
TRUE LOVE
A POWERFUL ENEMY
A REVEALING LETTER

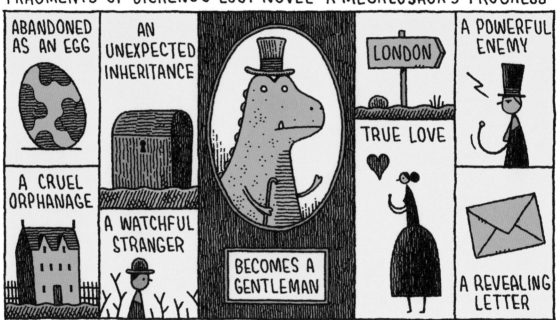

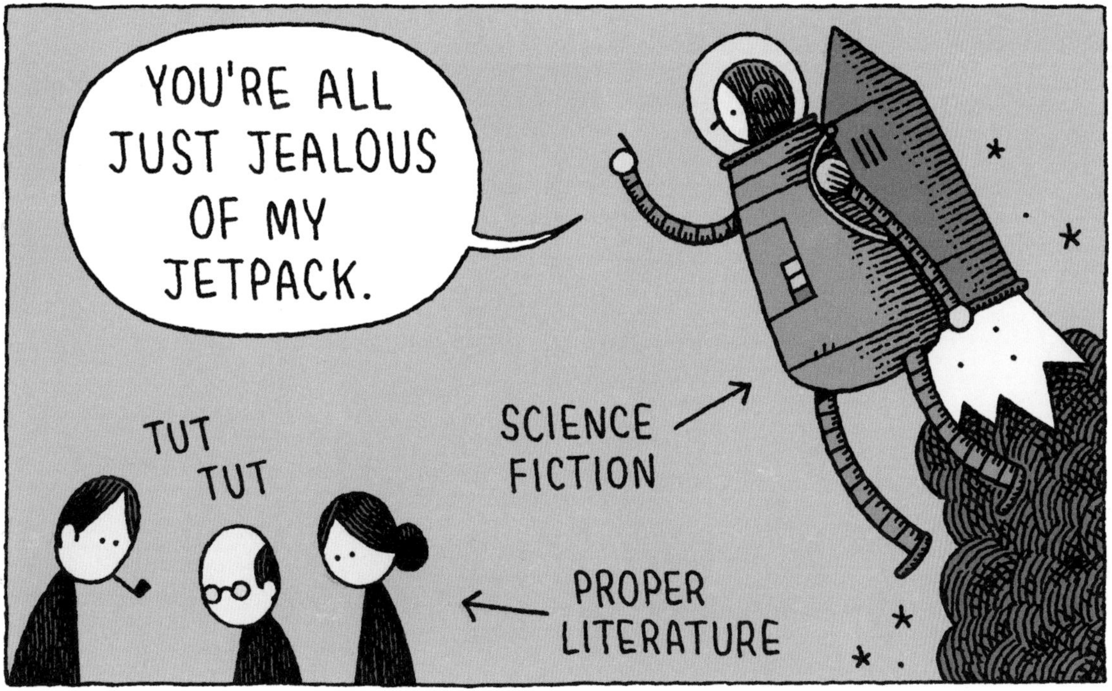
YOU'RE ALL JUST JEALOUS OF MY JETPACK.
SCIENCE FICTION
TUT TUT
PROPER LITERATURE

THE OWL AND THE SEASICK PUSSYCAT

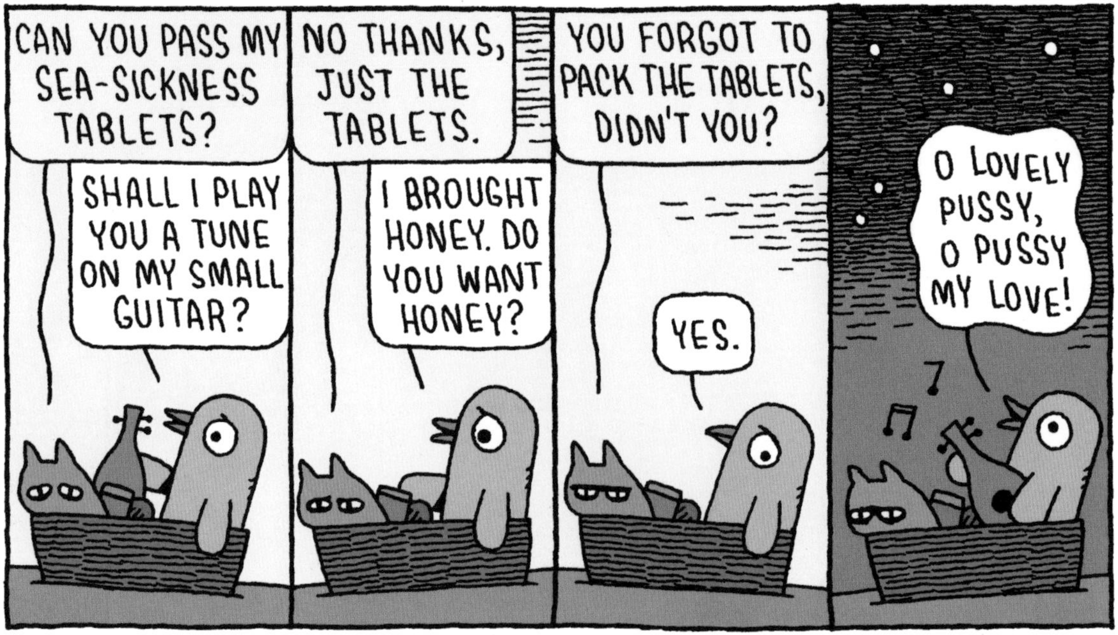
CAN YOU PASS MY SEA-SICKNESS TABLETS?
SHALL I PLAY YOU A TUNE ON MY SMALL GUITAR?
NO THANKS, JUST THE TABLETS.
I BROUGHT HONEY. DO YOU WANT HONEY?
YOU FORGOT TO PACK THE TABLETS, DIDN'T YOU?
YES.
O LOVELY PUSSY, O PUSSY MY LOVE!

COMING SOON: BRONTË SISTERS-THE VIDEOGAME

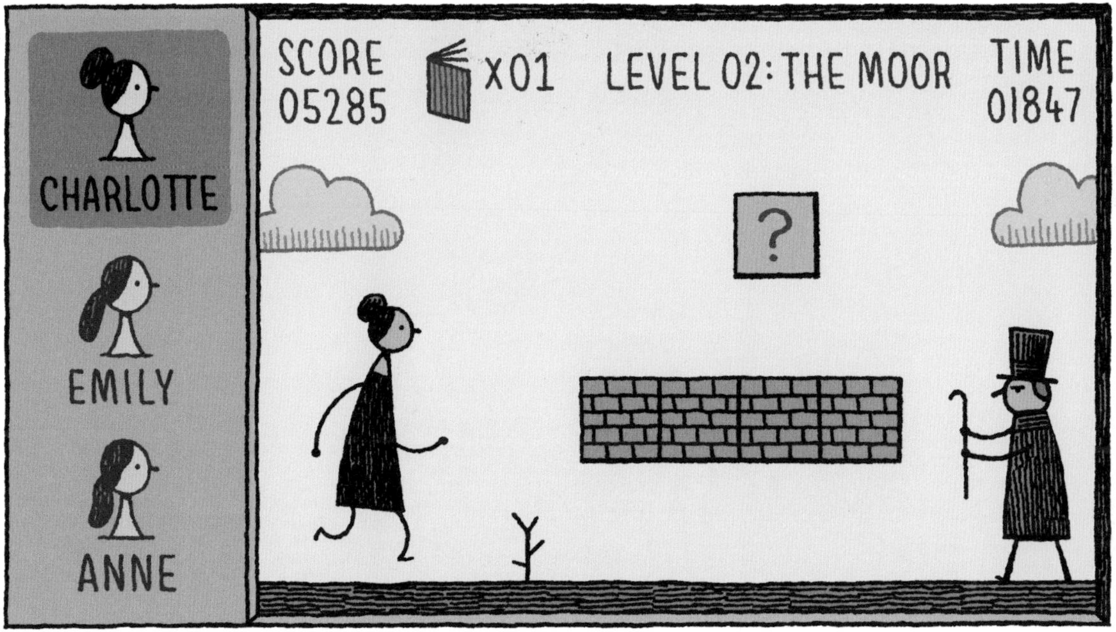

CHARLOTTE
EMILY
ANNE
SCORE
05285
X01
LEVEL 02: THE MOOR
TIME
01847
?

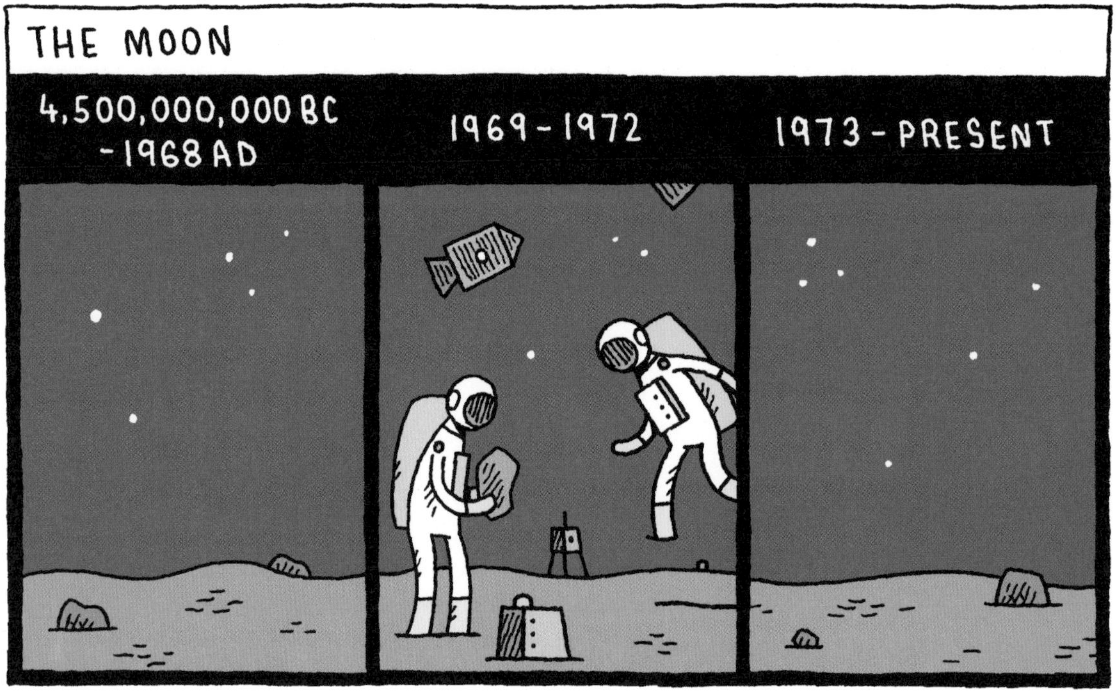
THE MOON
4,500,000,000 BC -1968 AD
1969 - 1972
1973 - PRESENT

THE GREAT AUTHOR CONSIDERS HIS RESPONSE TO THE QUESTION
SWEEPING GENERALIZATION
INSULT
STUNNING INSIGHT
RANT
UNRELATED ANECDOTE
JOKE
BIZARRE METAPHOR
ENIGMATIC SMILE
YES
NO
STRAIGHTFORWARD ANSWER

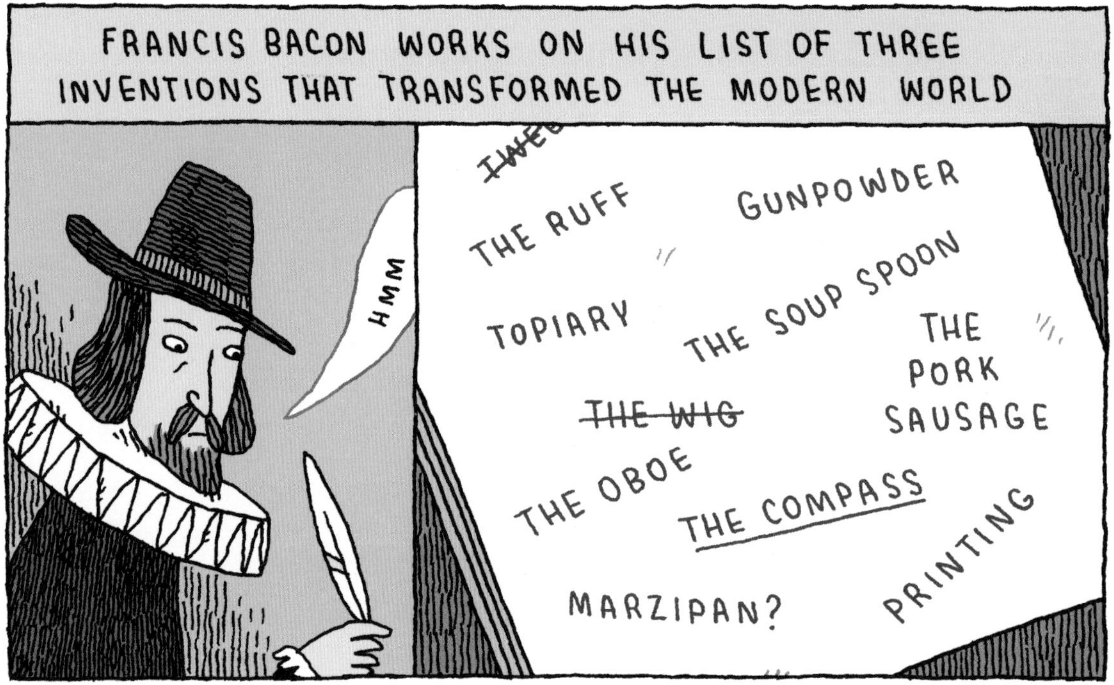
FRANCIS BACON WORKS ON HIS LIST OF THREE INVENTIONS THAT TRANSFORMED THE MODERN WORLD
HMM
THE RUFF
GUNPOWDER
TOPIARY
THE SOUP SPOON
THE PORK SAUSAGE
~~THE WIG~~
THE OBOE
THE COMPASS
MARZIPAN?
PRINTING

THE SERIOUS ROCK CRITIC
HUMBUG!
AHA! A YOUNGSTER. STEALING MUSIC NO DOUBT.
I'M COLLABORATING ONLINE WITH MUSICIANS ALL OVER THE GLOBE TO CREATE AN ELECTRONIC SYMPHONY.
I'VE WRITTEN 32 BOOKS ABOUT LED ZEPPELIN.
I'M QUITE BUSY ACTUALLY.
MICK FLEETWOOD ONCE FELL INTO MY POND...
CAN YOU GO AWAY NOW PLEASE.

DRUNK CLASSICS
GREAT LITERATURE
WITH ADDED BOOZE!

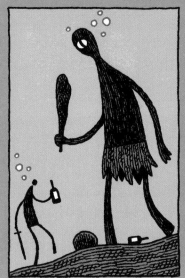

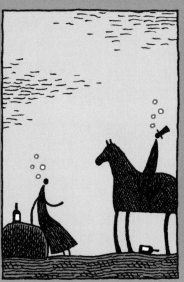

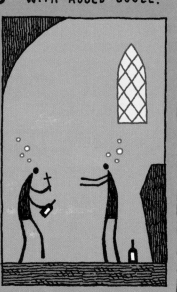

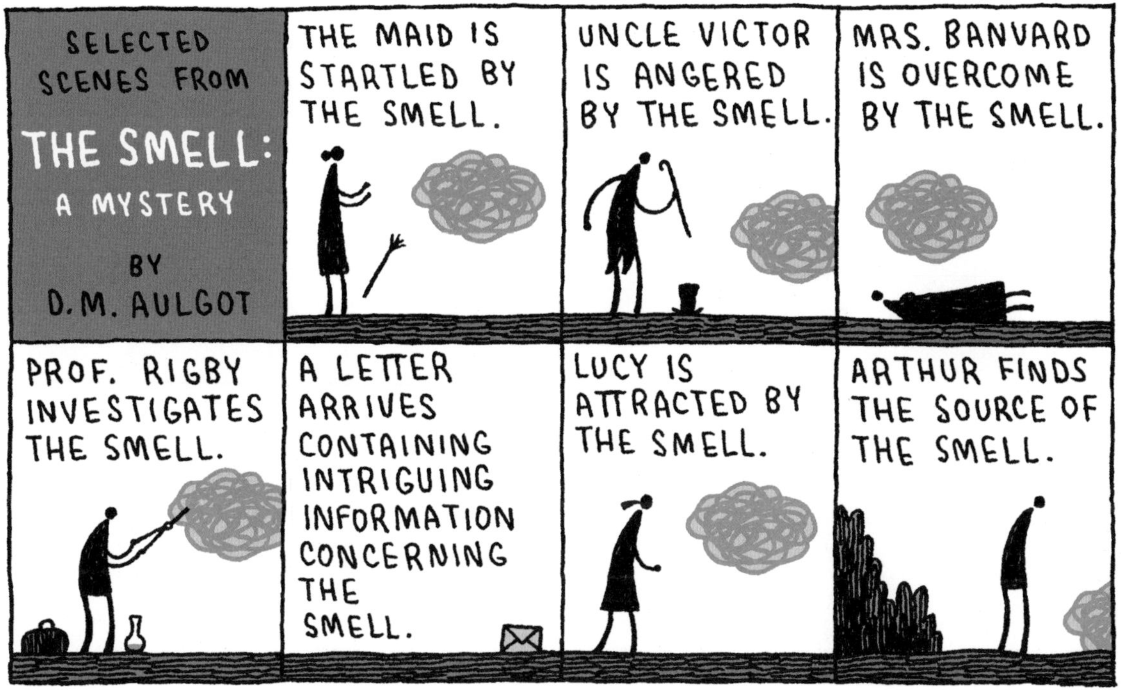

SELECTED SCENES FROM

THE SMELL:
A MYSTERY

BY
D.M. AULGOT

THE MAID IS STARTLED BY THE SMELL.

UNCLE VICTOR IS ANGERED BY THE SMELL.

MRS. BANVARD IS OVERCOME BY THE SMELL.

PROF. RIGBY INVESTIGATES THE SMELL.

A LETTER ARRIVES CONTAINING INTRIGUING INFORMATION CONCERNING THE SMELL.

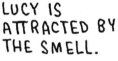

LUCY IS ATTRACTED BY THE SMELL.

ARTHUR FINDS THE SOURCE OF THE SMELL.

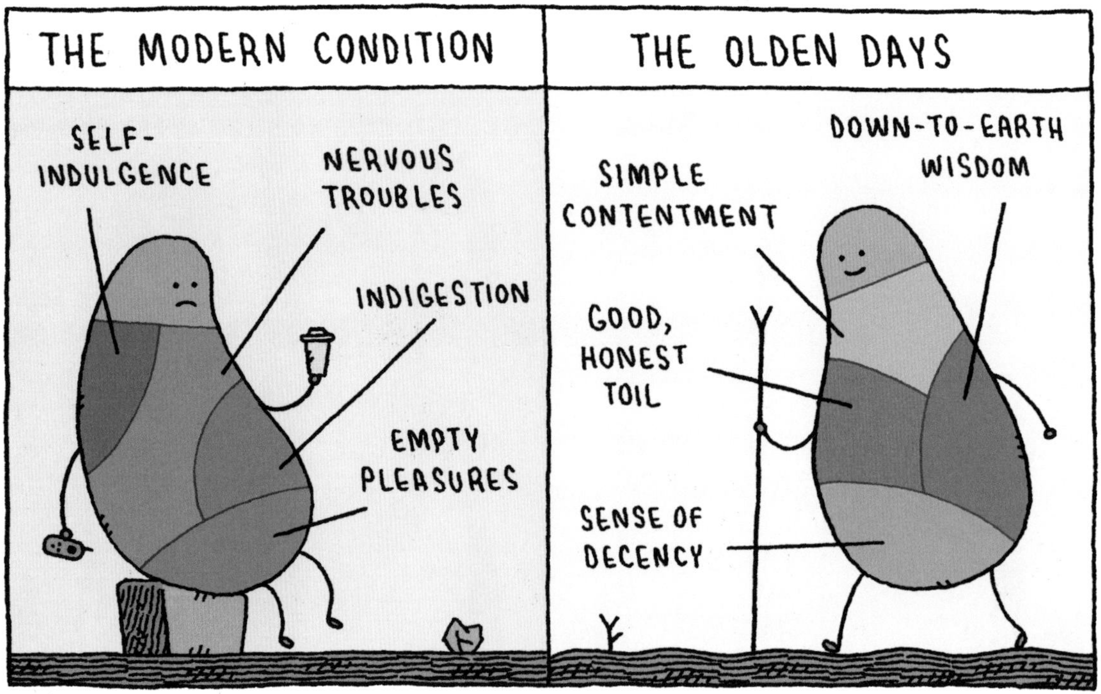

THE MODERN CONDITION
SELF-INDULGENCE
NERVOUS TROUBLES
INDIGESTION
EMPTY PLEASURES
THE OLDEN DAYS
SIMPLE CONTENTMENT
DOWN-TO-EARTH WISDOM
GOOD, HONEST TOIL
SENSE OF DECENCY

LOST SCENES FROM QUADROPHENIA

| WILD WEST INTERLUDE | THE MAGIC PEBBLE | DESTINATION MARS! |

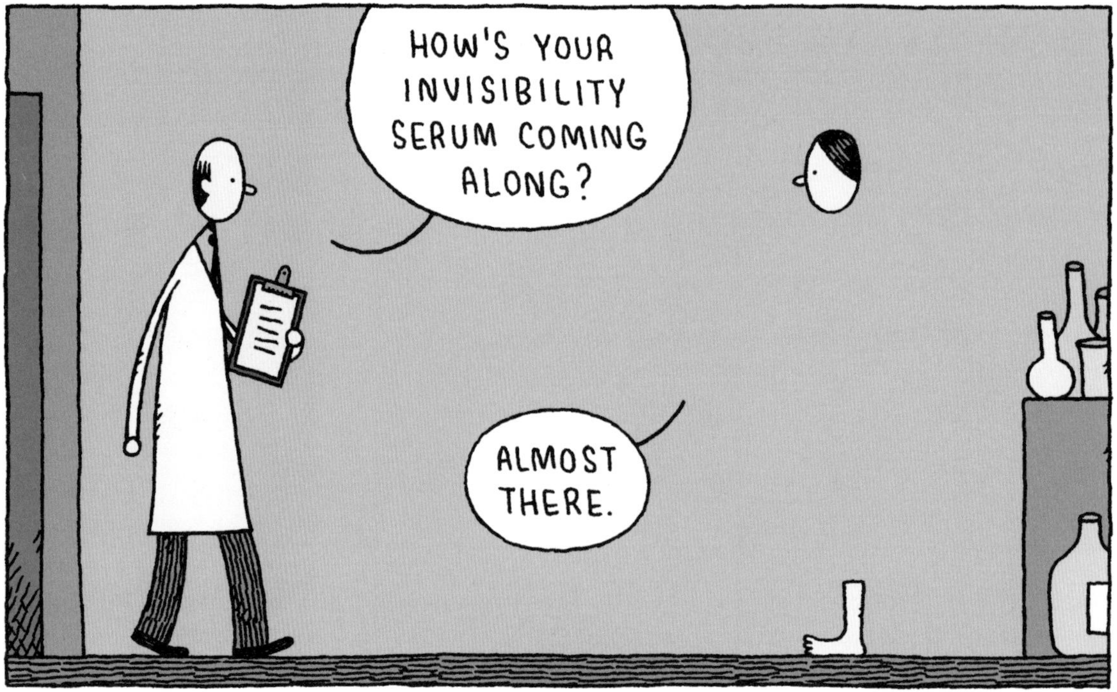
HOW'S YOUR INVISIBILITY SERUM COMING ALONG?
ALMOST THERE.

DO YOU HAVE STRONG FEELINGS ABOUT THE LEGACY OF THATCHERISM? WHY NOT EXPRESS THEM? ARRANGE THESE SYMBOLS TO CREATE A METAPHORICAL CARTOON! EXAMPLES BELOW.

THE GREEDY DOG STANDS ON THE CHAIR OF HOPE TO FEAST ON THE SAUSAGE OF HUBRIS.

THE AMBITIOUS SAUSAGE IS FREED FROM THE HUNGRY DOG BY THE CHAIR OF DEREGULATION.

THE DOG IS DEAD. THE CHAIR IS BROKEN. THE SAUSAGE IS COLD.

BEFORE DECIDING ON RATTY, MOLE AND MISTER TOAD, KENNETH GRAHAME TRIED SOME OTHER CHARACTERS

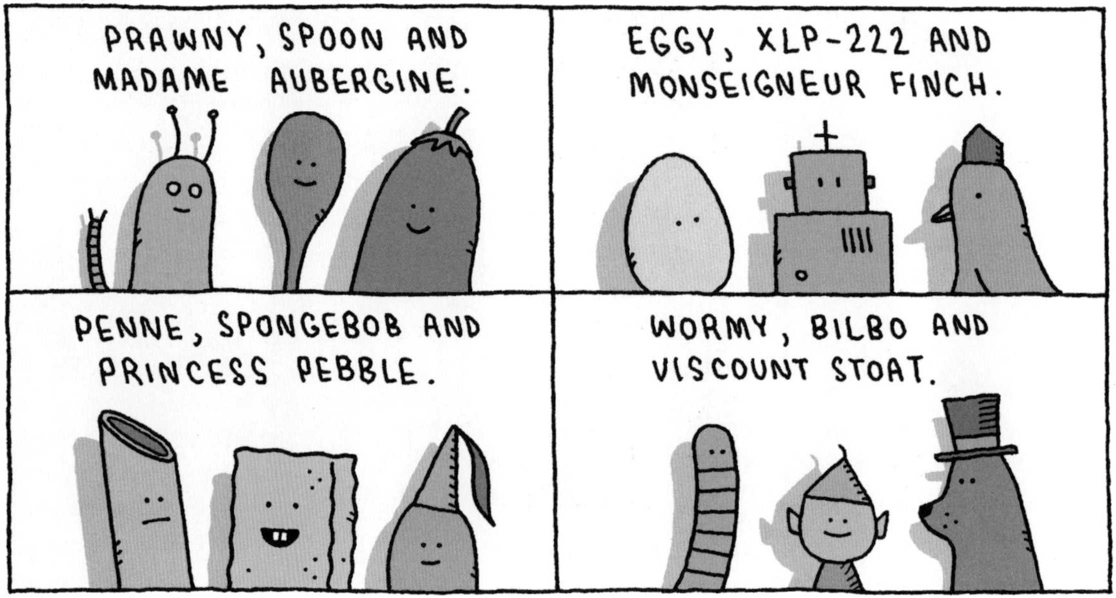
PRAWNY, SPOON AND MADAME AUBERGINE.
EGGY, XLP-222 AND MONSEIGNEUR FINCH.
PENNE, SPONGEBOB AND PRINCESS PEBBLE.
WORMY, BILBO AND VISCOUNT STOAT.

LARGE MARGHERITA FOR BLOOD CASTLE

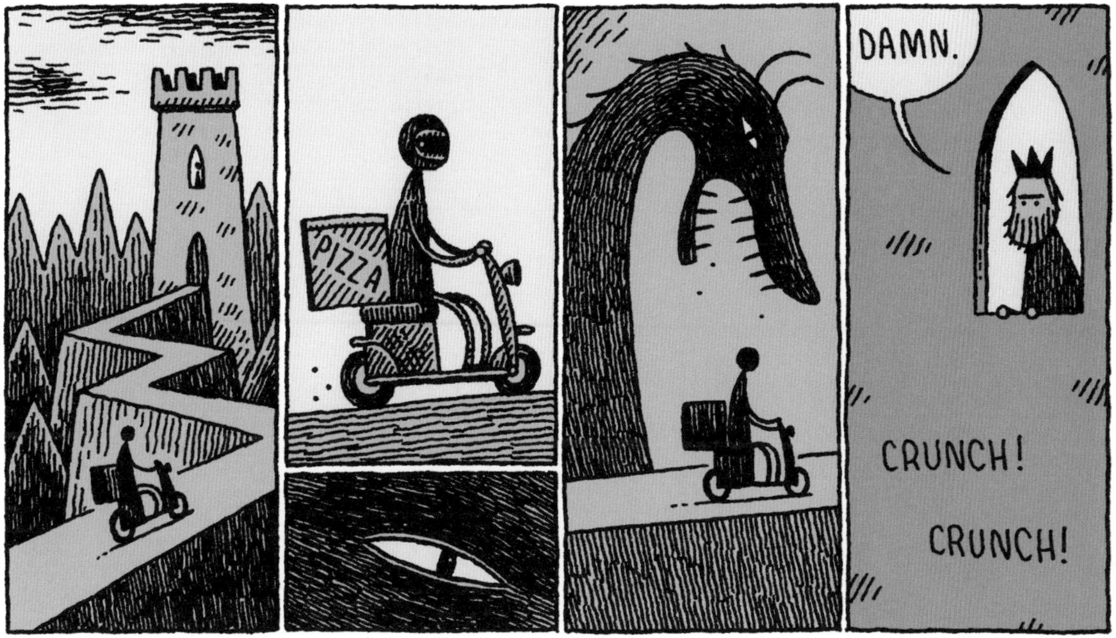
PIZZA
DAMN.
CRUNCH!
CRUNCH!

A SUNNY DAY IN THE PARK

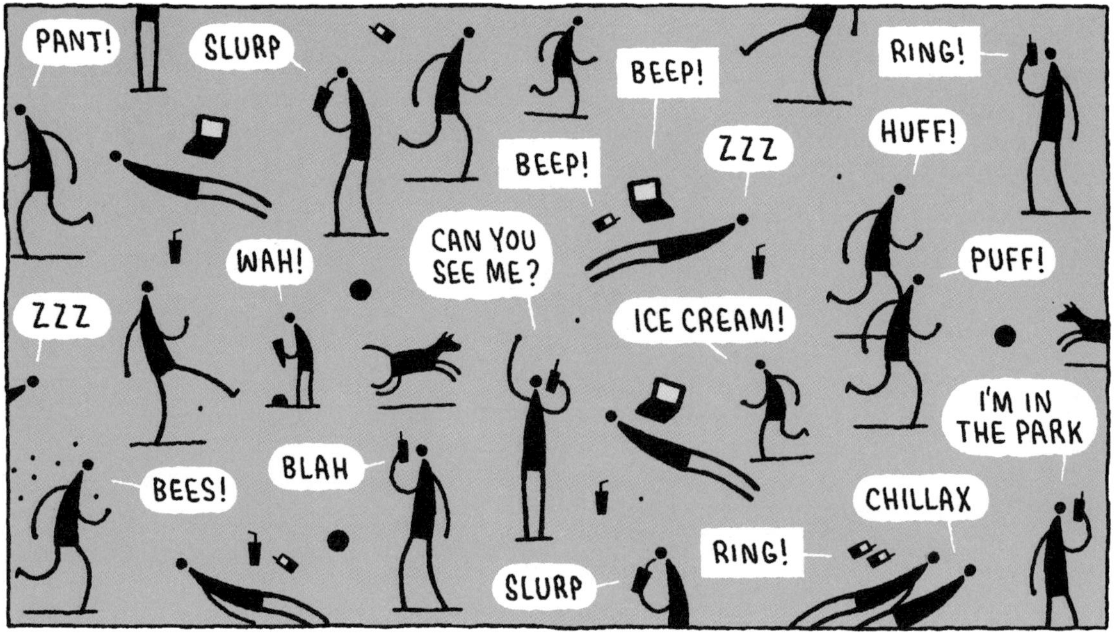
PANT!
SLURP
RING!
BEEP!
BEEP!
ZZZ
HUFF!
CAN YOU SEE ME?
WAH!
PUFF!
ZZZ
ICE CREAM!
I'M IN THE PARK
BLAH
BEES!
CHILLAX
RING!
SLURP

THE TIME-TRAVELLERS HAVE ARRIVED IN 1895

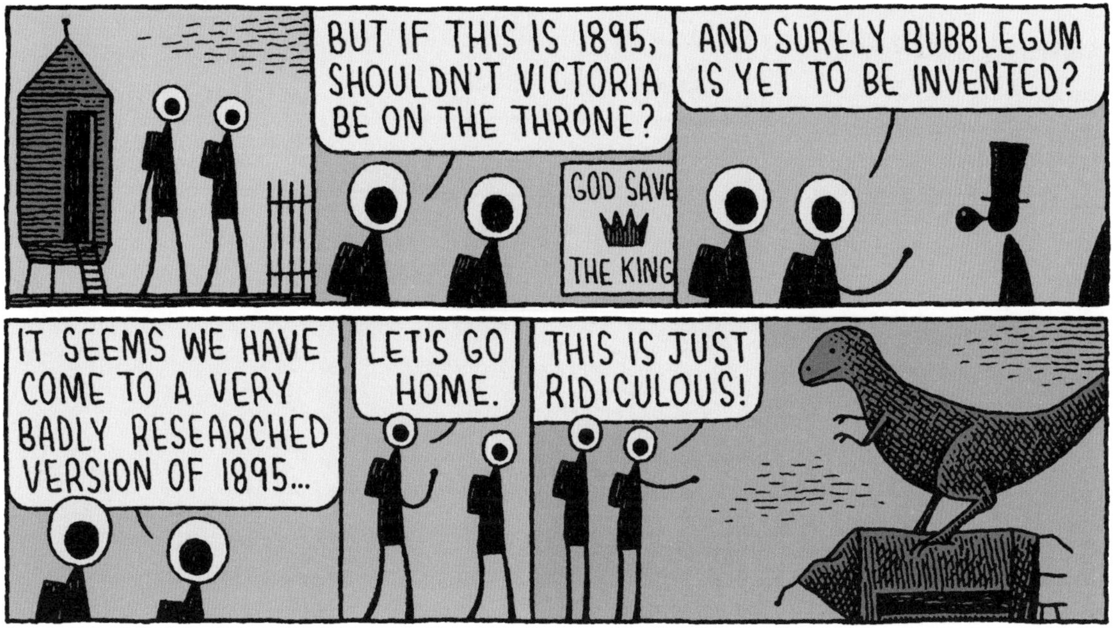
BUT IF THIS IS 1895, SHOULDN'T VICTORIA BE ON THE THRONE?
GOD SAVE
THE KING
AND SURELY BUBBLEGUM IS YET TO BE INVENTED?
IT SEEMS WE HAVE COME TO A VERY BADLY RESEARCHED VERSION OF 1895...
LET'S GO HOME.
THIS IS JUST RIDICULOUS!

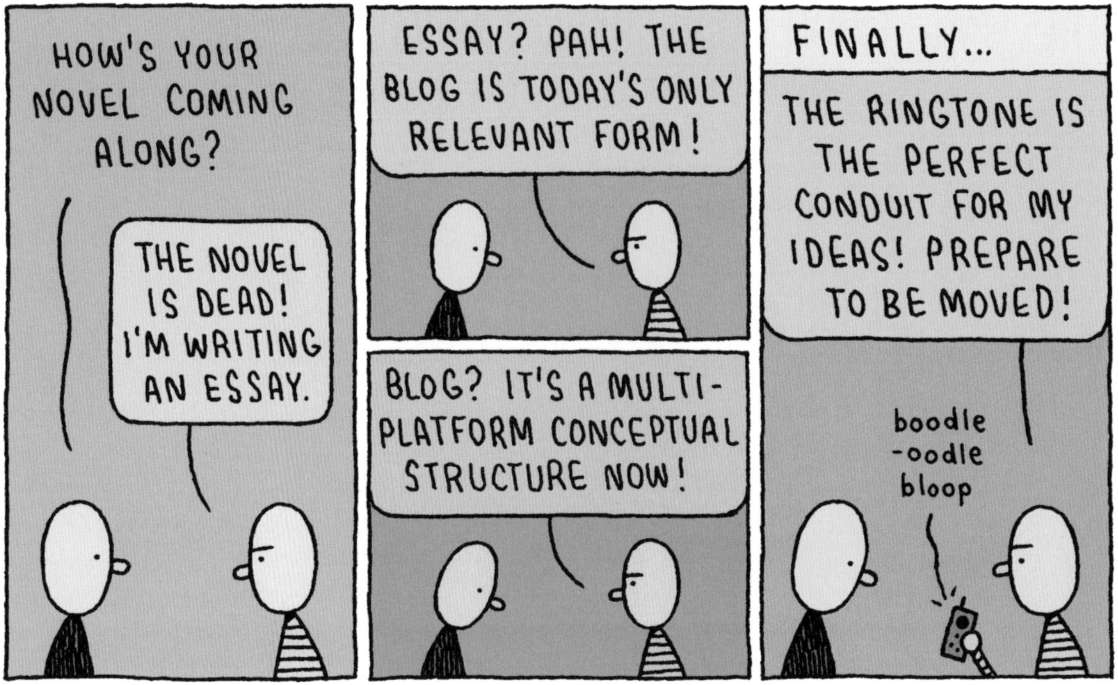
HOW'S YOUR NOVEL COMING ALONG?
THE NOVEL IS DEAD! I'M WRITING AN ESSAY.
ESSAY? PAH! THE BLOG IS TODAY'S ONLY RELEVANT FORM!
BLOG? IT'S A MULTI-PLATFORM CONCEPTUAL STRUCTURE NOW!
FINALLY...
THE RINGTONE IS THE PERFECT CONDUIT FOR MY IDEAS! PREPARE TO BE MOVED!
boodle -oodle bloop

Samuel Beckett's ADVENTURES OF TINTIN

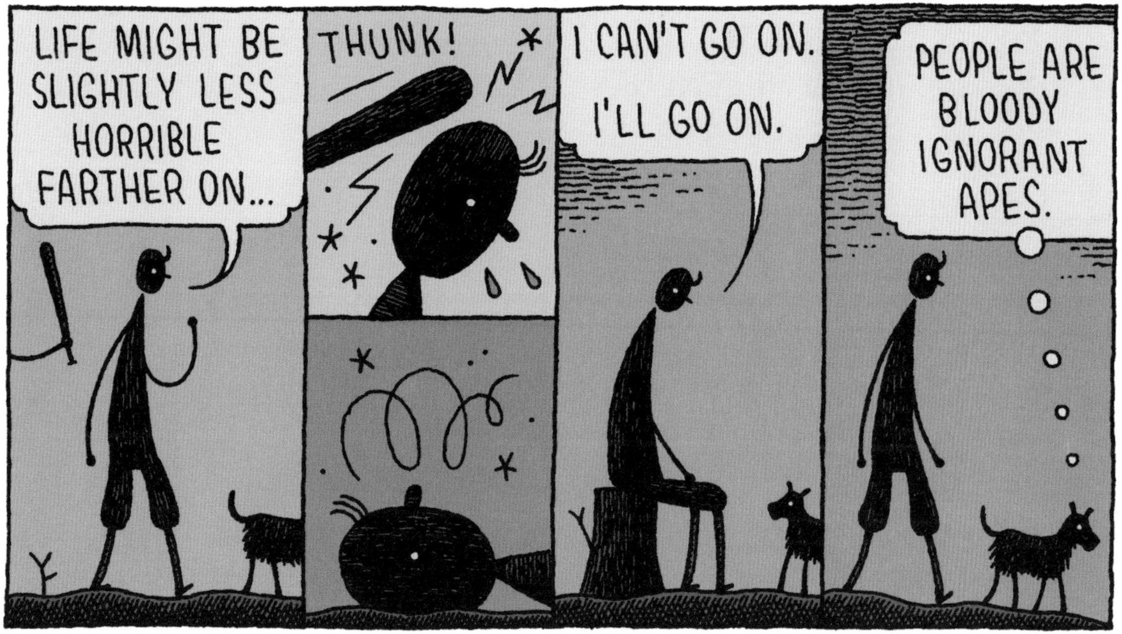
LIFE MIGHT BE SLIGHTLY LESS HORRIBLE FARTHER ON...
THUNK!
I CAN'T GO ON.
I'LL GO ON.
PEOPLE ARE BLOODY IGNORANT APES.

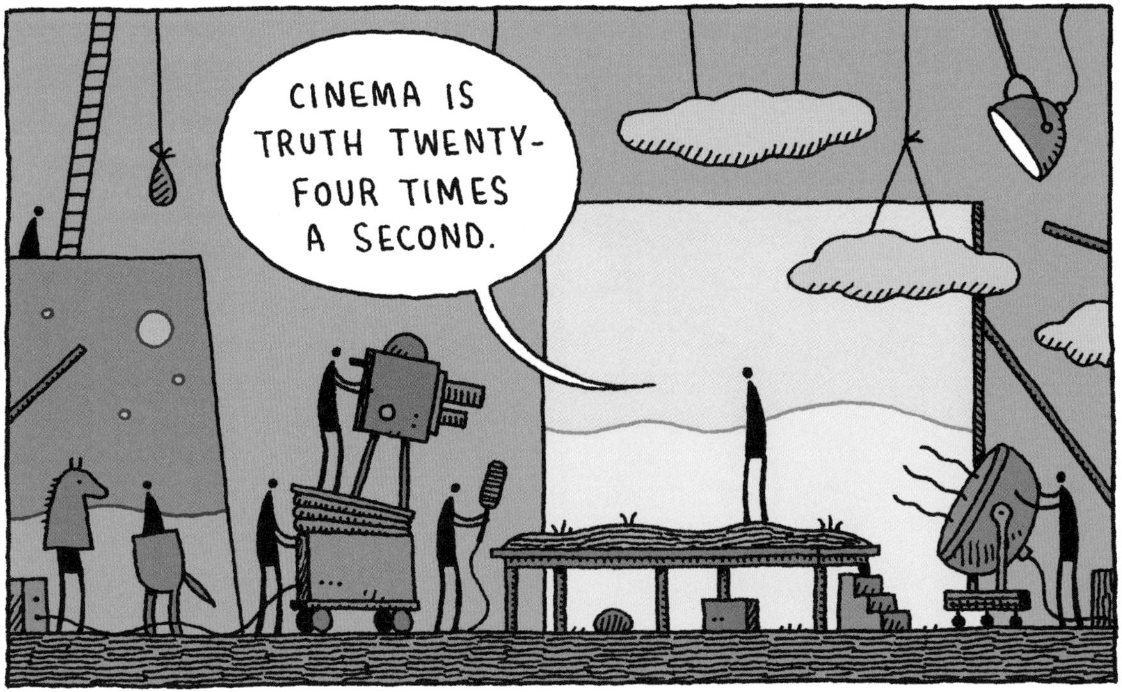
CINEMA IS TRUTH TWENTY-FOUR TIMES A SECOND.

HOMES of the FUTURE
2020
MINIMALIST CUBOID
2050
PROTECTIVE DOME
2080
UNDERGROUND BUNKER
2110
HUT IN THE FOREST
2140
CRYSTAL CITADEL
2170
SPACE PYRAMID
2200
THE NINTH DIMENSION

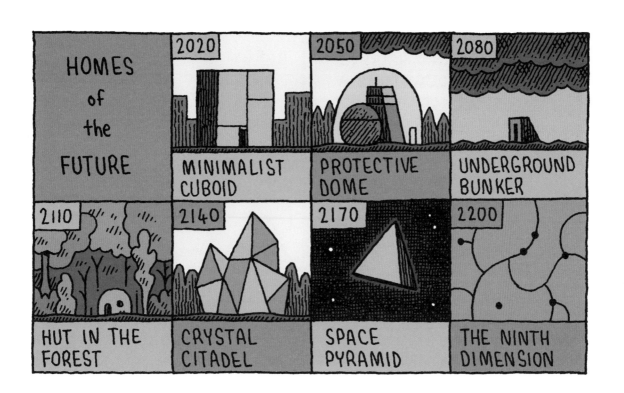

OH BOY! I CAN'T BELIEVE I'VE BEEN BOUGHT BY A FAMOUS WRITER! I CAN'T WAIT TO GET STARTED ON OUR MASTERPIECE!
A FEW DAYS LATER...

SOME OF THE THINGS THAT WE WILL BE ADDING IN THE MOVIE VERSION OF YOUR NOVEL
LONG-LOST TWIN
EXPLOSIONS
PARIS HILTON
DANCE ROUTINE
DREAM SEQUENCE
LOVABLE ORANGUTAN
HAPPY ENDING

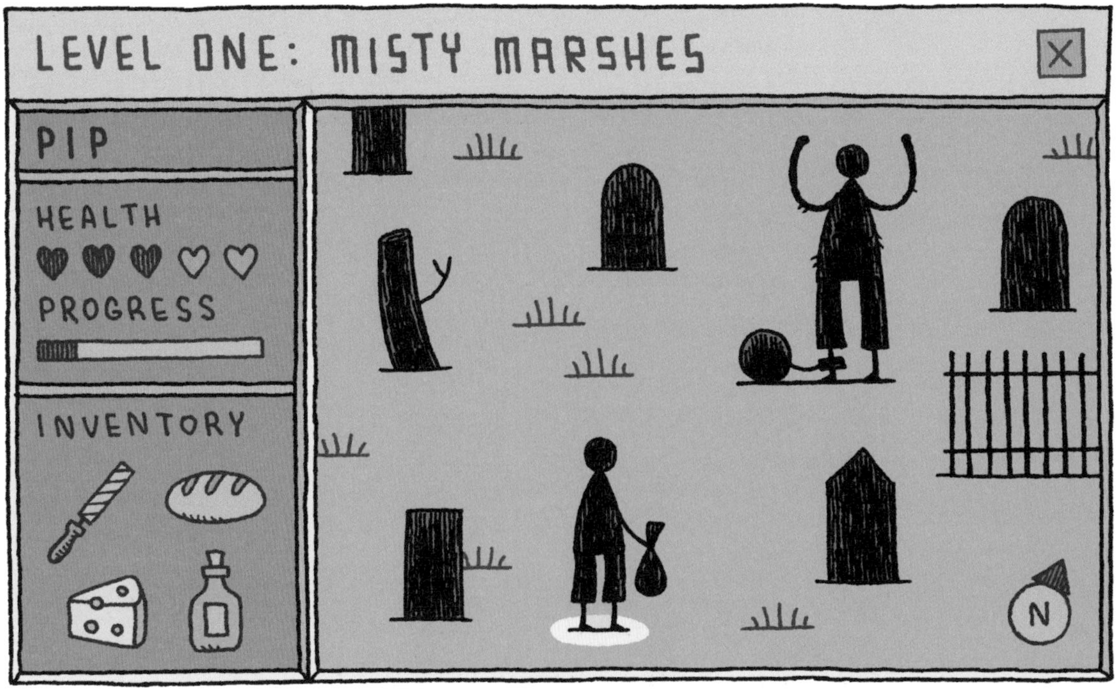
LEVEL ONE: MISTY MARSHES
X
PIP
HEALTH
PROGRESS
INVENTORY
N

MAO DISCUSSES THE 'LITTLE RED BOOK' WITH HIS EDITOR

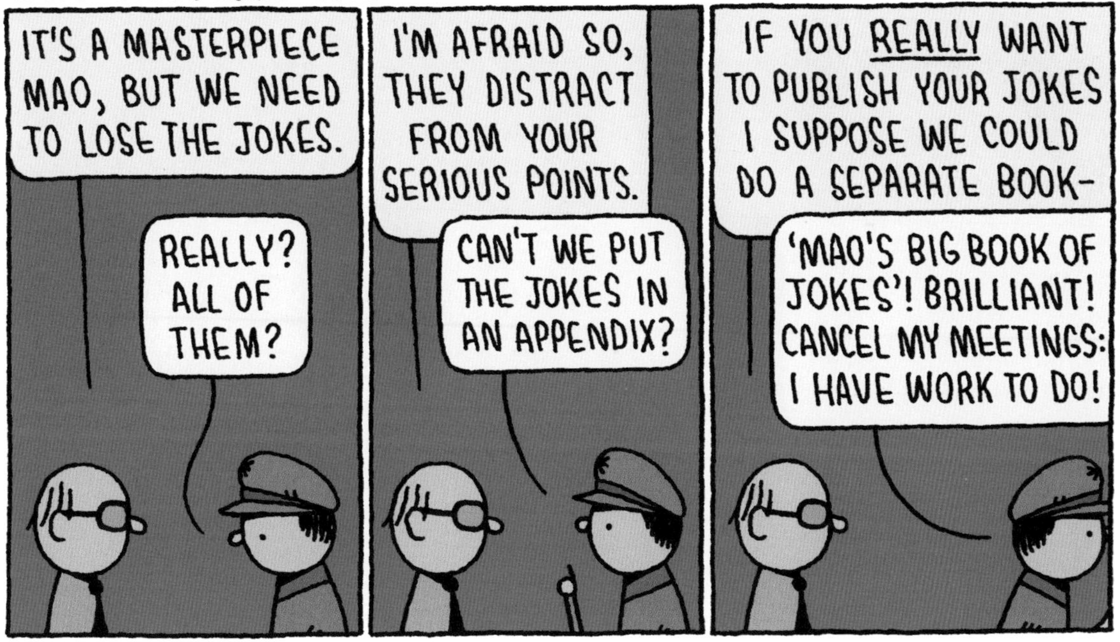
IT'S A MASTERPIECE MAO, BUT WE NEED TO LOSE THE JOKES.
REALLY? ALL OF THEM?
I'M AFRAID SO, THEY DISTRACT FROM YOUR SERIOUS POINTS.
CAN'T WE PUT THE JOKES IN AN APPENDIX?
IF YOU REALLY WANT TO PUBLISH YOUR JOKES I SUPPOSE WE COULD DO A SEPARATE BOOK-
'MAO'S BIG BOOK OF JOKES'! BRILLIANT! CANCEL MY MEETINGS: I HAVE WORK TO DO!

PHILIP PULLMAN IS OUT WALKING WHEN THE LORD SPEAKS TO HIM

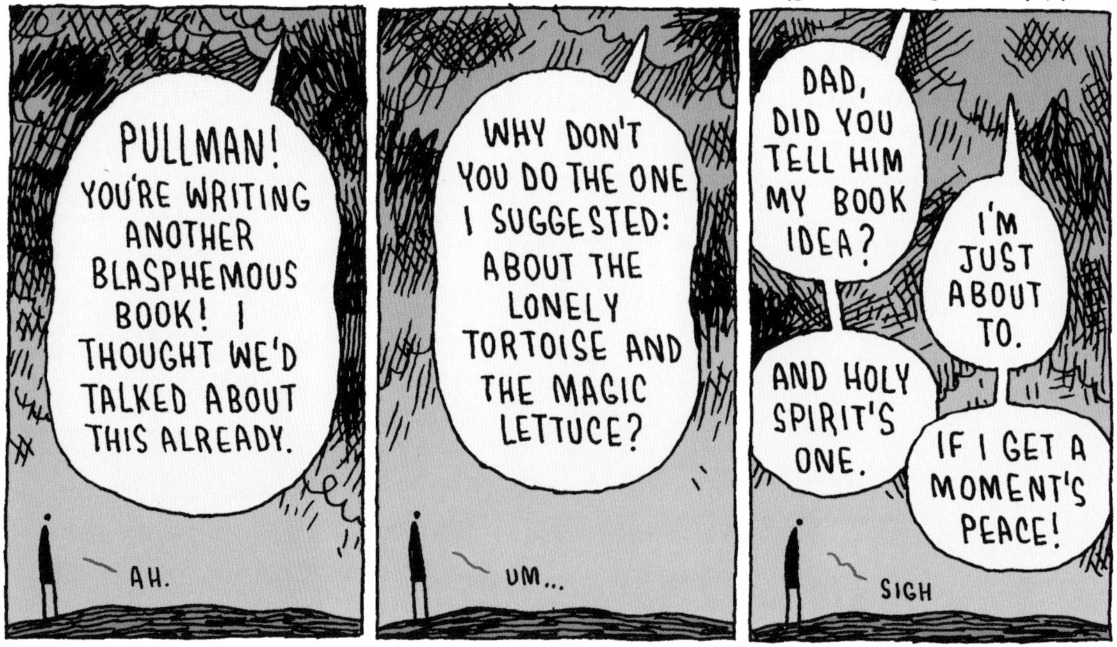
PULLMAN! YOU'RE WRITING ANOTHER BLASPHEMOUS BOOK! I THOUGHT WE'D TALKED ABOUT THIS ALREADY.
AH.
WHY DON'T YOU DO THE ONE I SUGGESTED: ABOUT THE LONELY TORTOISE AND THE MAGIC LETTUCE?
UM...
DAD, DID YOU TELL HIM MY BOOK IDEA?
I'M JUST ABOUT TO.
AND HOLY SPIRIT'S ONE.
IF I GET A MOMENT'S PEACE!
SIGH

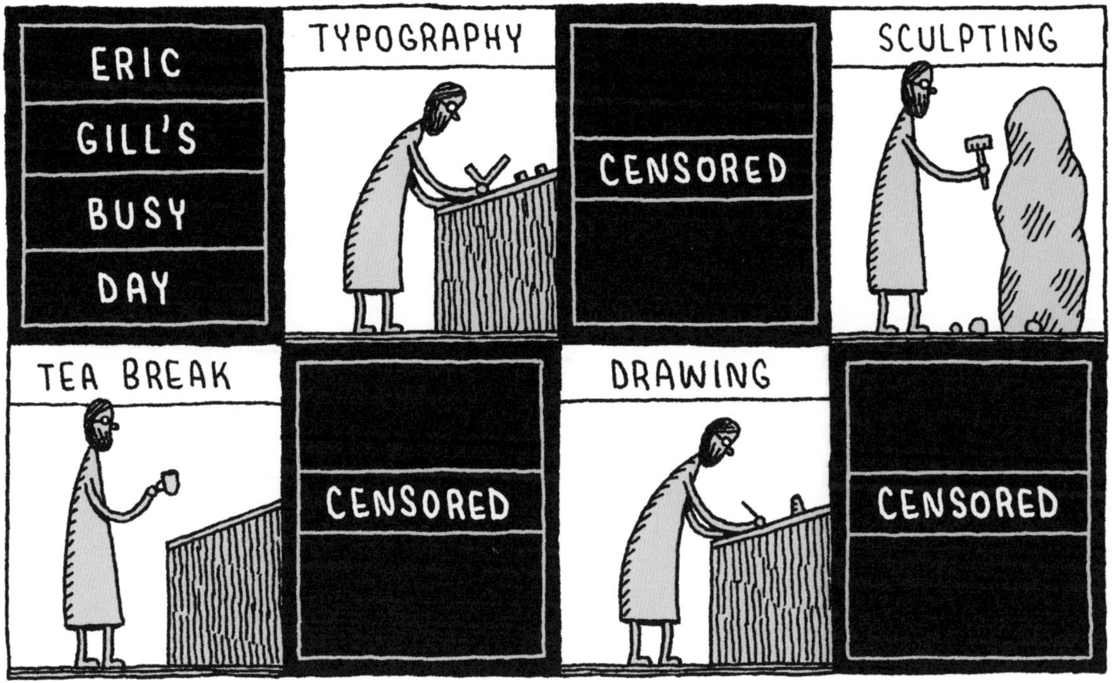
ERIC GILL'S BUSY DAY
TYPOGRAPHY
CENSORED
SCULPTING
TEA BREAK
CENSORED
DRAWING
CENSORED

SERVANTS IN AN UPPER-CLASS HOUSEHOLD

USUAL

BUTLER

VALET

LADY'S MAID

GARDENER

COOK

LESS USUAL

BARBARIAN

CHILD CATCHER

I.T. SUPPORT

GHOSTBUSTER

DOMINATRIX

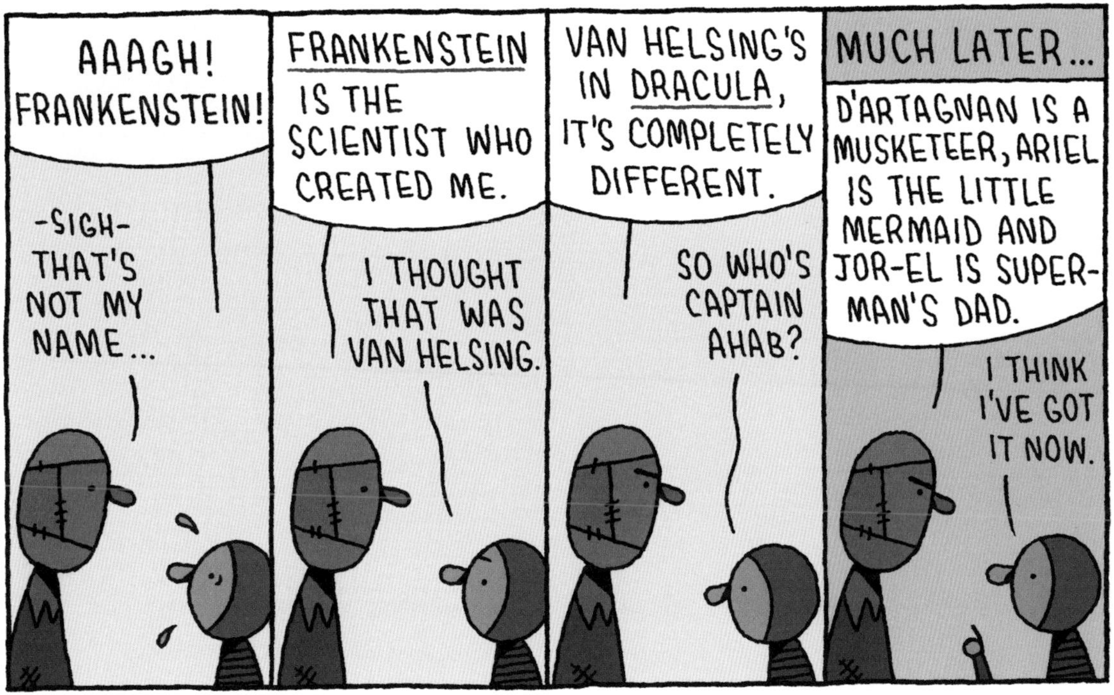
AAAGH! FRANKENSTEIN!
-SIGH- THAT'S NOT MY NAME...
FRANKENSTEIN IS THE SCIENTIST WHO CREATED ME.
I THOUGHT THAT WAS VAN HELSING.
VAN HELSING'S IN DRACULA, IT'S COMPLETELY DIFFERENT.
SO WHO'S CAPTAIN AHAB?
MUCH LATER...
D'ARTAGNAN IS A MUSKETEER, ARIEL IS THE LITTLE MERMAID AND JOR-EL IS SUPER-MAN'S DAD.
I THINK I'VE GOT IT NOW.

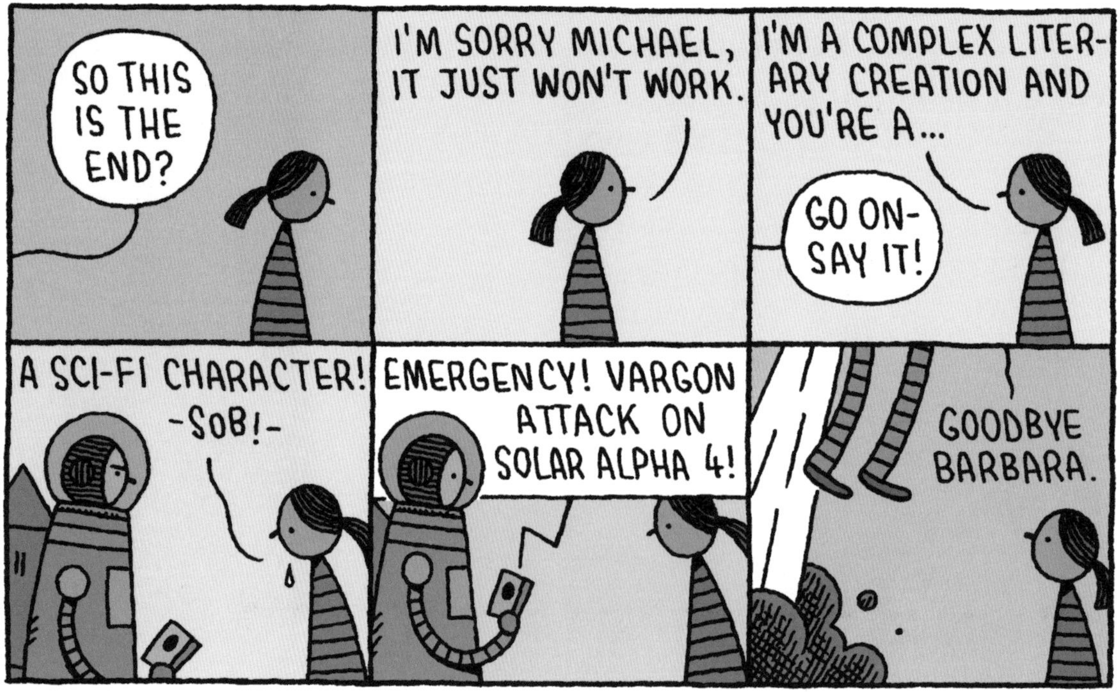
SO THIS IS THE END?
I'M SORRY MICHAEL, IT JUST WON'T WORK.
I'M A COMPLEX LITERARY CREATION AND YOU'RE A...
GO ON- SAY IT!
A SCI-FI CHARACTER!
-SOB!-
EMERGENCY! VARGON ATTACK ON SOLAR ALPHA 4!
GOODBYE BARBARA.

NEW YEAR'S RESOLUTION: WORSHIP A MADE-UP GOD

LORD BORAX   URT   HAAHOŪ   UNIT333

ONCE THERE WAS AN INCOMPLETE CROSSWORD

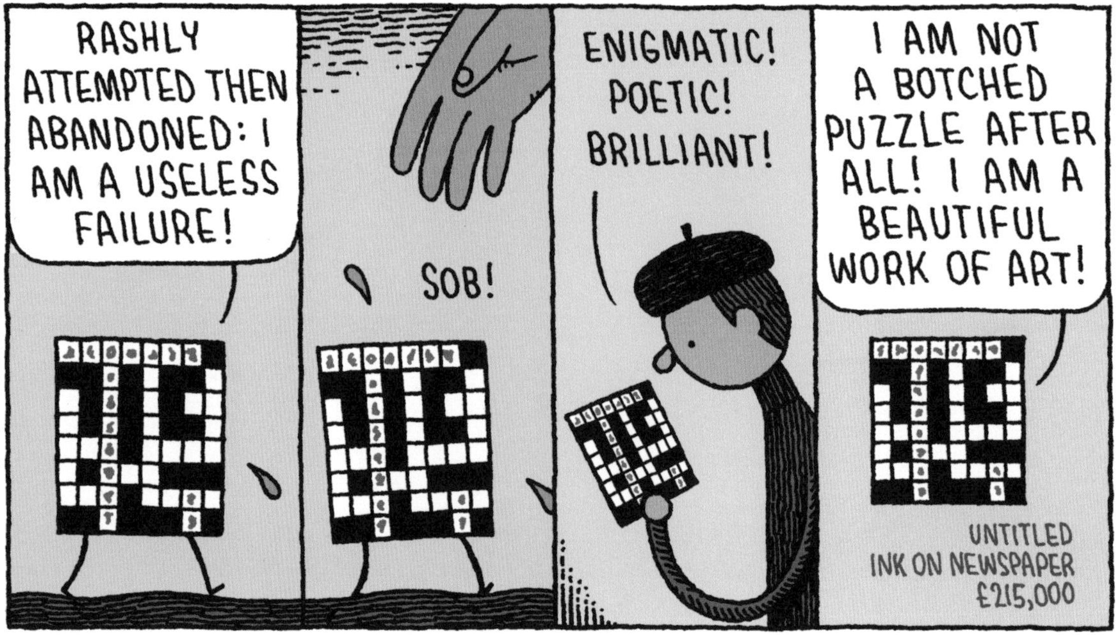
RASHLY ATTEMPTED THEN ABANDONED: I AM A USELESS FAILURE!
SOB!
ENIGMATIC! POETIC! BRILLIANT!
I AM NOT A BOTCHED PUZZLE AFTER ALL! I AM A BEAUTIFUL WORK OF ART!
UNTITLED
INK ON NEWSPAPER
£215,000

THE SHAKESPEARE CONSPIRACY
PREVIOUSLY: THE PROFESSOR CALCULATED THAT SHAKESPEARE'S PLAYS WERE WRITTEN ON THE MOON. ROGERS AND SIMPSON HAVE BEEN SENT TO INVESTIGATE...
INSIDE THE PYRAMID
DAN BROWN!
YES! I WROTE THEM!! AND THERE'S NOTHING YOU CAN DO ABOUT IT!
NO!
NOOO!
HA HA HA!
HE'S GETTING AWAY!
HA! HA!!
THE END..?

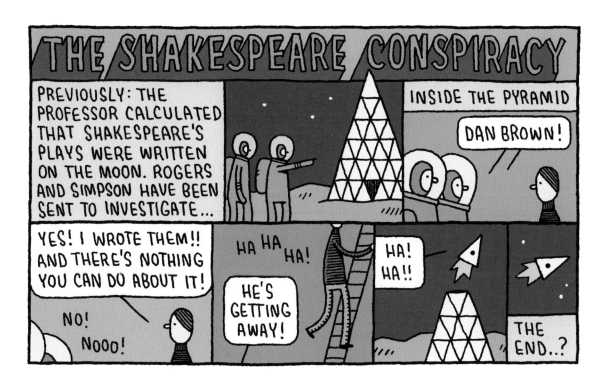

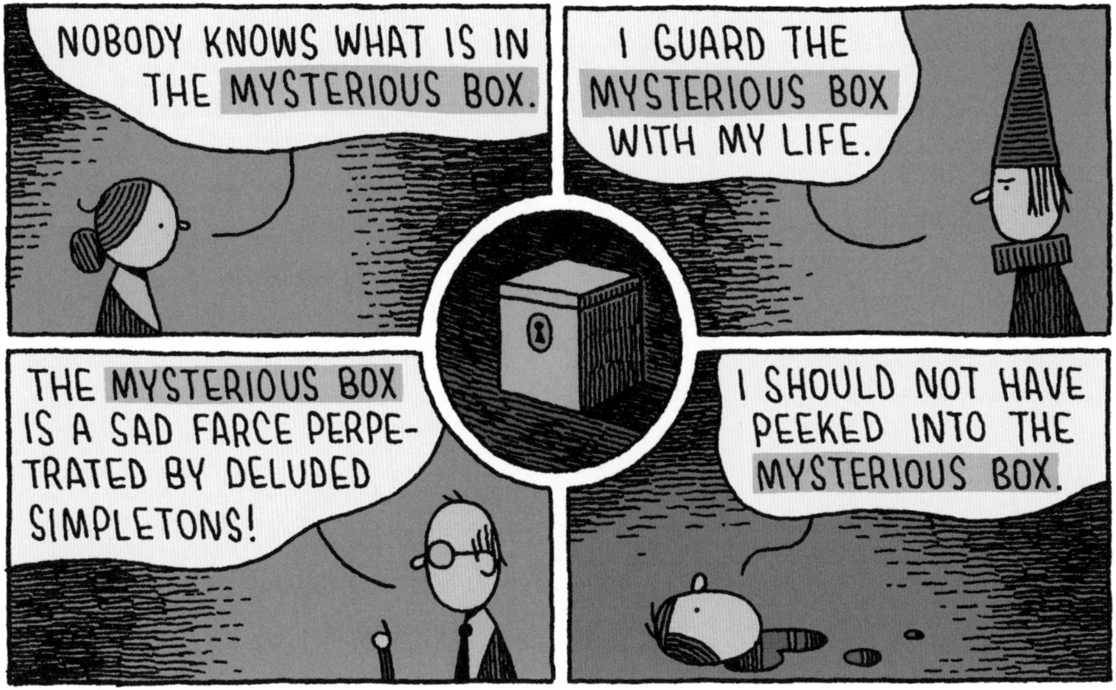
NOBODY KNOWS WHAT IS IN THE MYSTERIOUS BOX.
I GUARD THE MYSTERIOUS BOX WITH MY LIFE.
THE MYSTERIOUS BOX IS A SAD FARCE PERPETRATED BY DELUDED SIMPLETONS!
I SHOULD NOT HAVE PEEKED INTO THE MYSTERIOUS BOX.

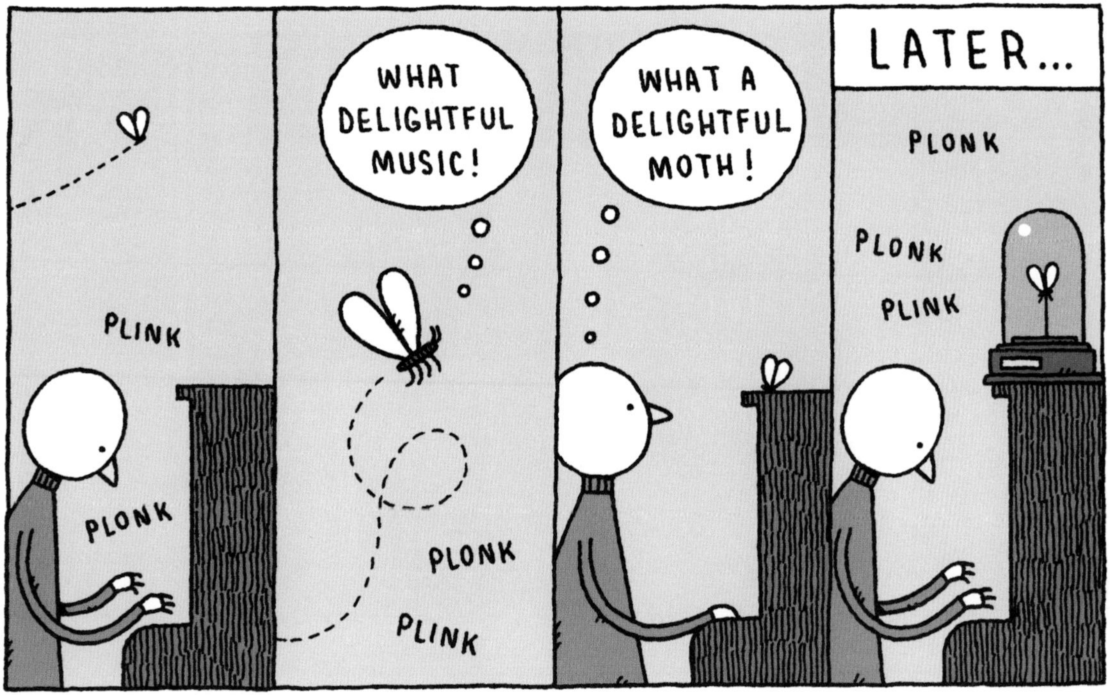

PLINK
PLONK
WHAT DELIGHTFUL MUSIC!
PLONK
PLINK
WHAT A DELIGHTFUL MOTH!
LATER...
PLONK
PLONK
PLINK

LONDON'S FIRST UNDERGROUND RAILWAY WAS BUILT BY CHARLES DICKENS TO AID HIS CRIME-FIGHTING ACTIVITIES...
THE DICKENSMOBILE.
MAP OF THE TUNNELS.
N
DICKENS IN ACTION!

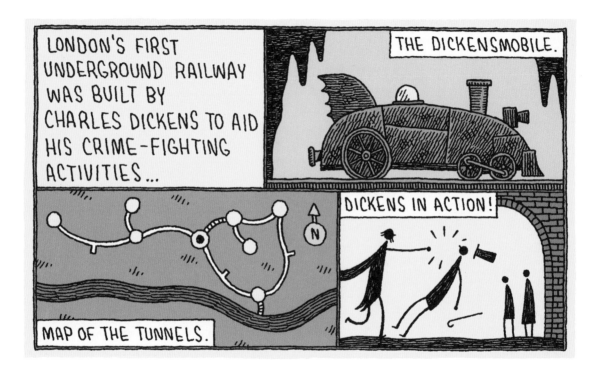

THE UNORPHANED CHILDREN'S BOOK HEROINE

SALLY MUST JOIN OUR QUEST. ONLY SHE CAN DEFEAT THE WITCH-QUEEN OF MORDAX.
NOT TILL SHE EATS UP HER BROCCOLI.

IF YOU LIKE URBAN MUSIC YOU MAY ALSO ENJOY:

DORMITORY
TOWN FUNK

HISTORIC
VILLAGE
METAL

BUSINESS
DISTRICT
INDIE-POP

DESIGNATED
REDEVELOP-
MENT ZONE
JAZZ

SMALL RETAIL
PARK BLUES

GREENBELT
ELECTRONICA

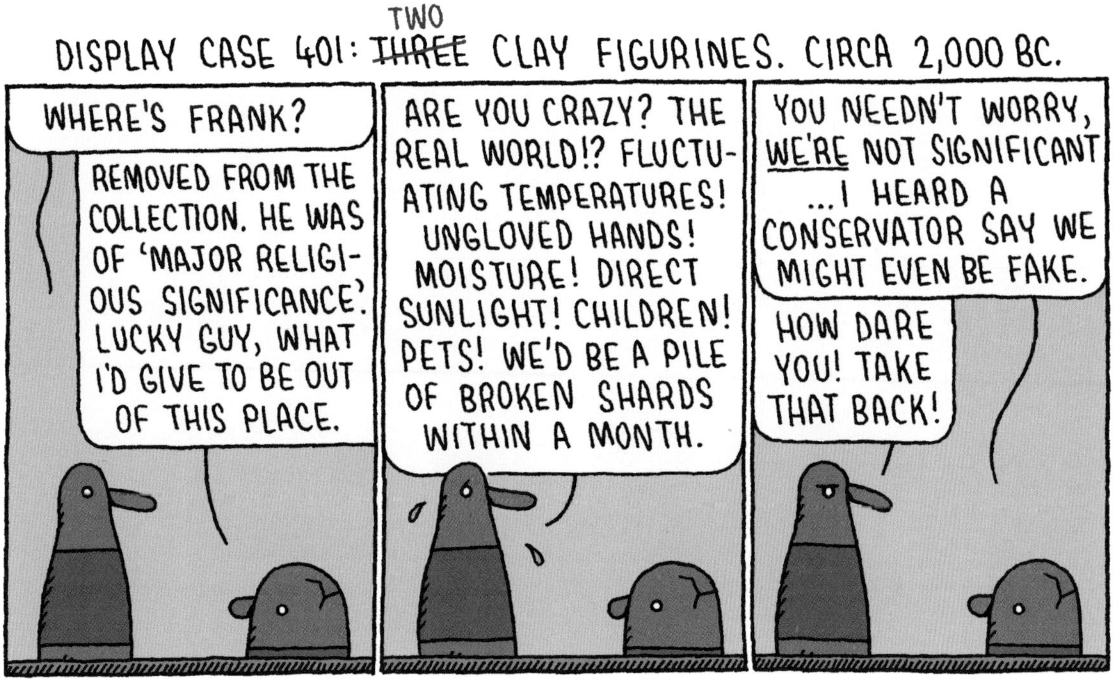
DISPLAY CASE 401: ~~THREE~~ TWO CLAY FIGURINES. CIRCA 2,000 BC.
WHERE'S FRANK?
REMOVED FROM THE COLLECTION. HE WAS OF 'MAJOR RELIGIOUS SIGNIFICANCE'. LUCKY GUY, WHAT I'D GIVE TO BE OUT OF THIS PLACE.
ARE YOU CRAZY? THE REAL WORLD!? FLUCTUATING TEMPERATURES! UNGLOVED HANDS! MOISTURE! DIRECT SUNLIGHT! CHILDREN! PETS! WE'D BE A PILE OF BROKEN SHARDS WITHIN A MONTH.
YOU NEEDN'T WORRY, WE'RE NOT SIGNIFICANT ...I HEARD A CONSERVATOR SAY WE MIGHT EVEN BE FAKE.
HOW DARE YOU! TAKE THAT BACK!

EVOLUTION OF THE POETRY RECEPTACLE

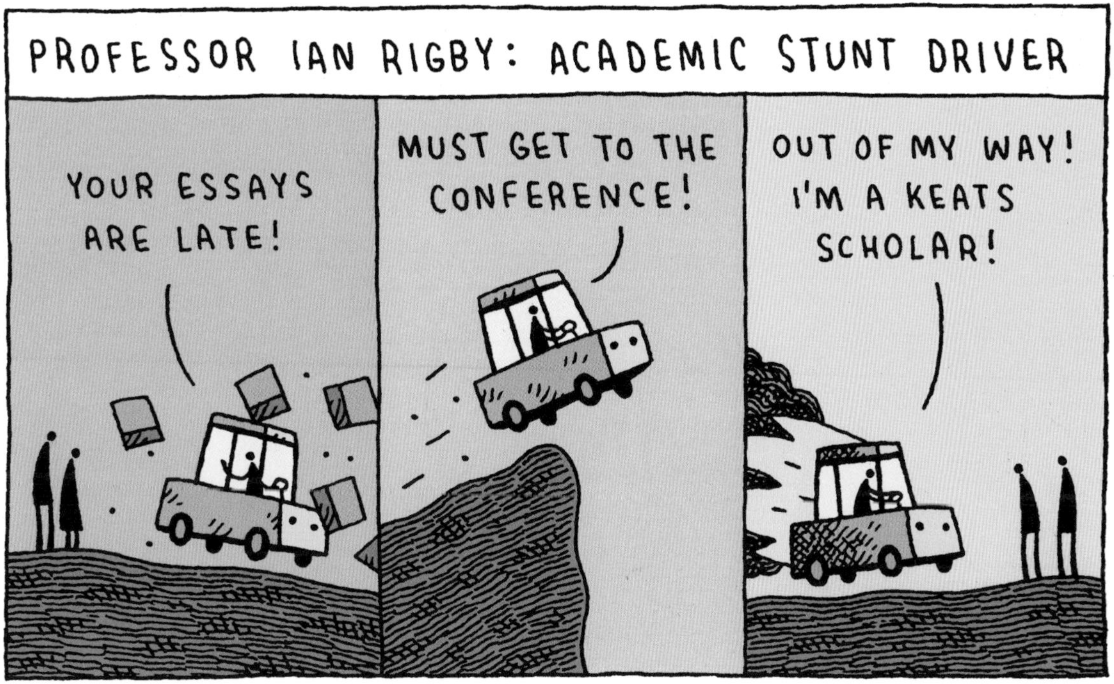
PROFESSOR IAN RIGBY: ACADEMIC STUNT DRIVER
YOUR ESSAYS ARE LATE!
MUST GET TO THE CONFERENCE!
OUT OF MY WAY! I'M A KEATS SCHOLAR!

2042 AD: SCIENCE AND RELIGION DECIDE TO PUT ASIDE THEIR DIFFERENCES AND FORM A PARTNERSHIP.

A FIERCE WAR BREAKS OUT BETWEEN THOSE WHO WANT TO NAME THE HYBRID 'RIENCE' AND THOSE WHO PREFER 'SELIGION'.

2049 AD: IT IS AGREED THAT THINGS WERE BETTER BEFORE. RELIGION AND SCIENCE GO THEIR SEPARATE WAYS.

CRICKET BOOKS
A TECHNICAL HISTORY OF CRICKET
A VIOLENT HISTORY OF CRICKET
A FUTURE HISTORY OF CRICKET
A SOCIAL HISTORY OF CRICKET
A SURREAL HISTORY OF CRICKET
A HEROIC HISTORY OF CRICKET

THE INDECISIVE NOVELIST'S CHARACTERS CONVERSE

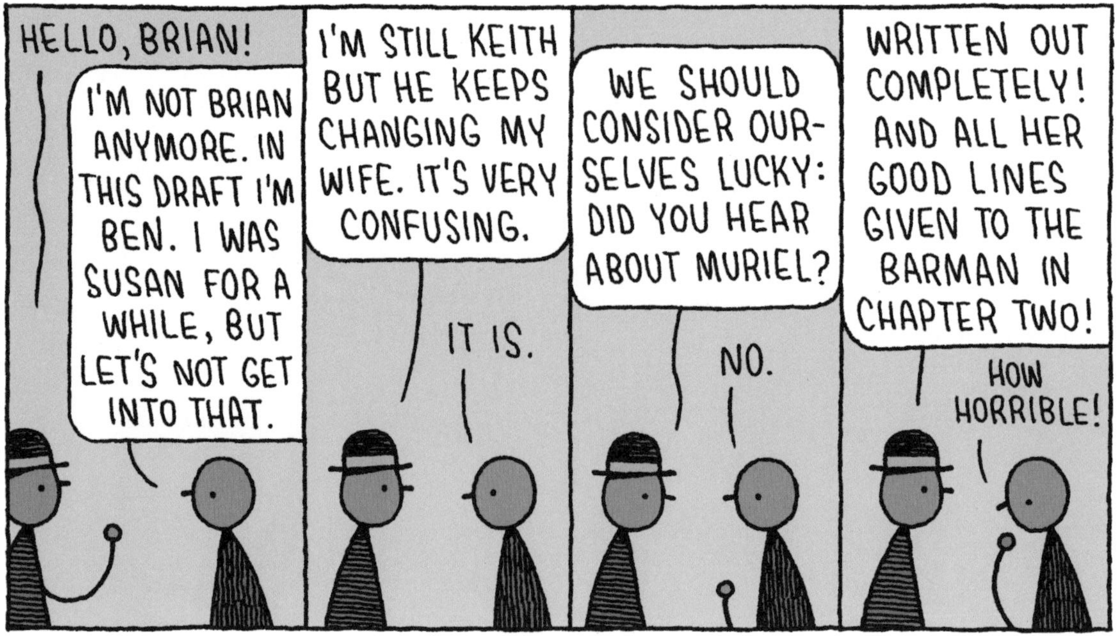
HELLO, BRIAN!
I'M NOT BRIAN ANYMORE. IN THIS DRAFT I'M BEN. I WAS SUSAN FOR A WHILE, BUT LET'S NOT GET INTO THAT.
I'M STILL KEITH BUT HE KEEPS CHANGING MY WIFE. IT'S VERY CONFUSING.
IT IS.
WE SHOULD CONSIDER OUR-SELVES LUCKY: DID YOU HEAR ABOUT MURIEL?
NO.
WRITTEN OUT COMPLETELY! AND ALL HER GOOD LINES GIVEN TO THE BARMAN IN CHAPTER TWO!
HOW HORRIBLE!

OH DEAR!

THE MUSICAL INSTRUMENTS ARE ALL MIXED UP.

CAN YOU MATCH THEM WITH THEIR FAMOUS OWNERS?

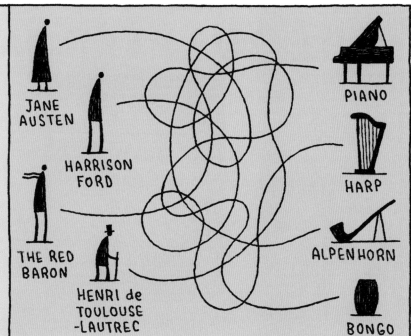

JANE AUSTEN

HARRISON FORD

THE RED BARON

HENRI de TOULOUSE -LAUTREC

PIANO

HARP

ALPENHORN

BONGO

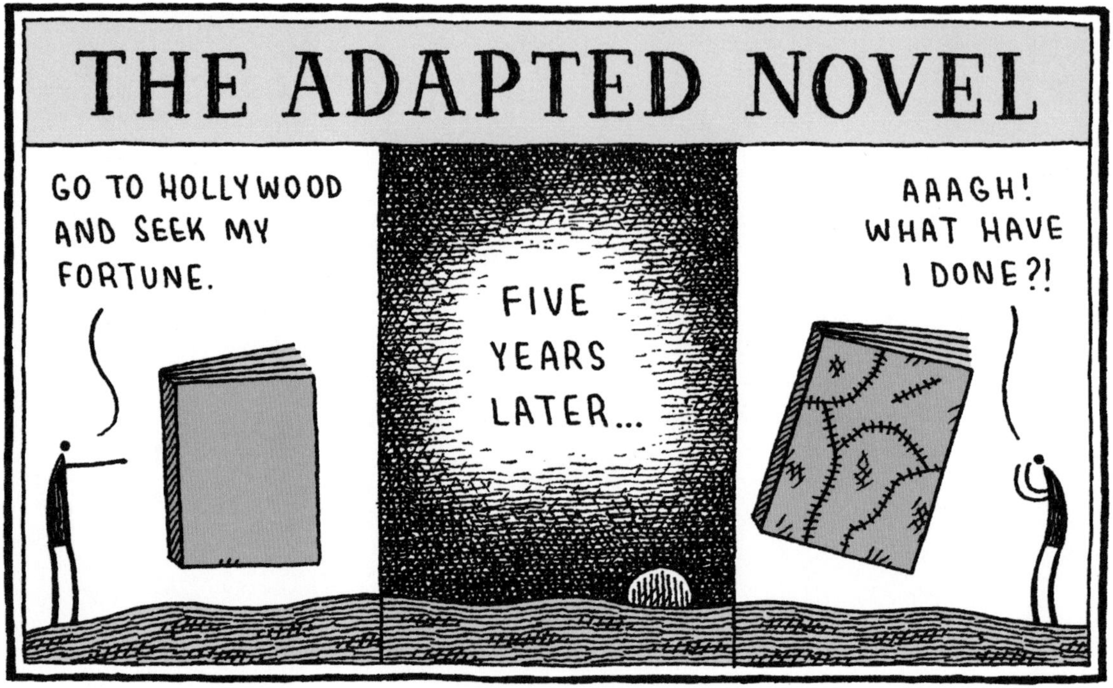
THE ADAPTED NOVEL
GO TO HOLLYWOOD AND SEEK MY FORTUNE.
FIVE YEARS LATER...
AAAGH! WHAT HAVE I DONE?!

A MOUSE RECALLS PULLING CINDERELLA'S CARRIAGE

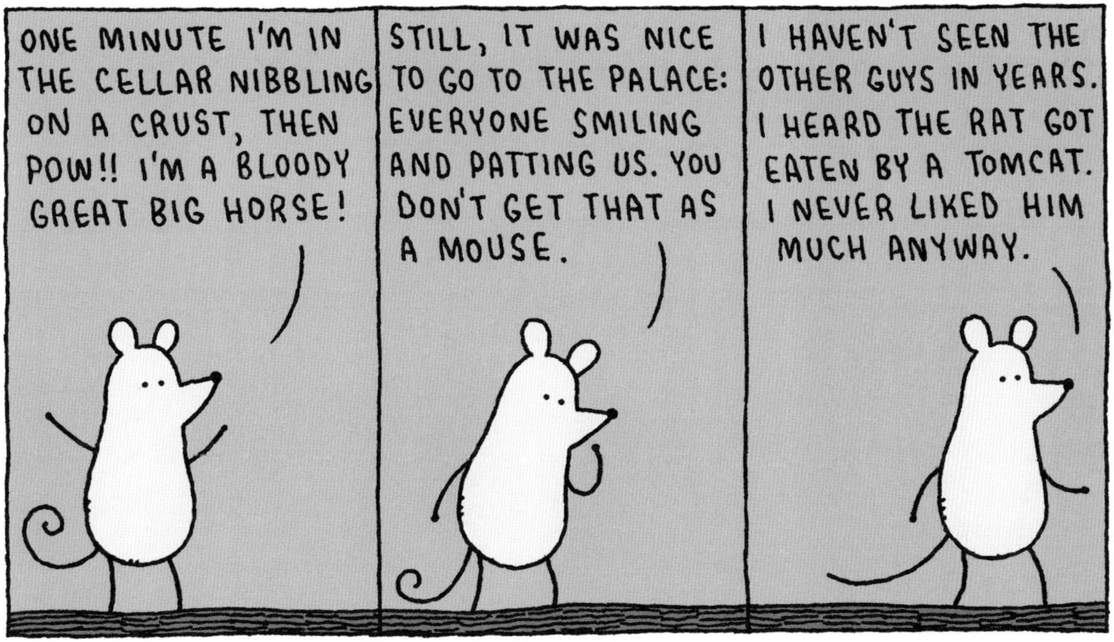
ONE MINUTE I'M IN THE CELLAR NIBBLING ON A CRUST, THEN POW!! I'M A BLOODY GREAT BIG HORSE!
STILL, IT WAS NICE TO GO TO THE PALACE: EVERYONE SMILING AND PATTING US. YOU DON'T GET THAT AS A MOUSE.
I HAVEN'T SEEN THE OTHER GUYS IN YEARS. I HEARD THE RAT GOT EATEN BY A TOMCAT. I NEVER LIKED HIM MUCH ANYWAY.

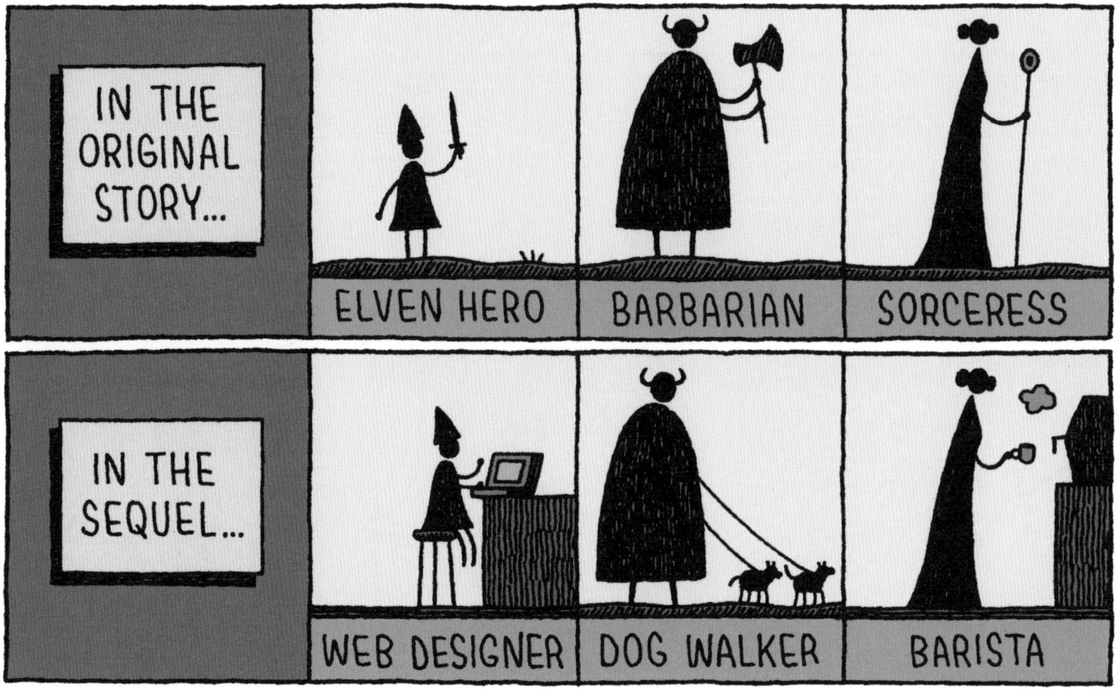
IN THE ORIGINAL STORY...
ELVEN HERO
BARBARIAN
SORCERESS
IN THE SEQUEL...
WEB DESIGNER
DOG WALKER
BARISTA

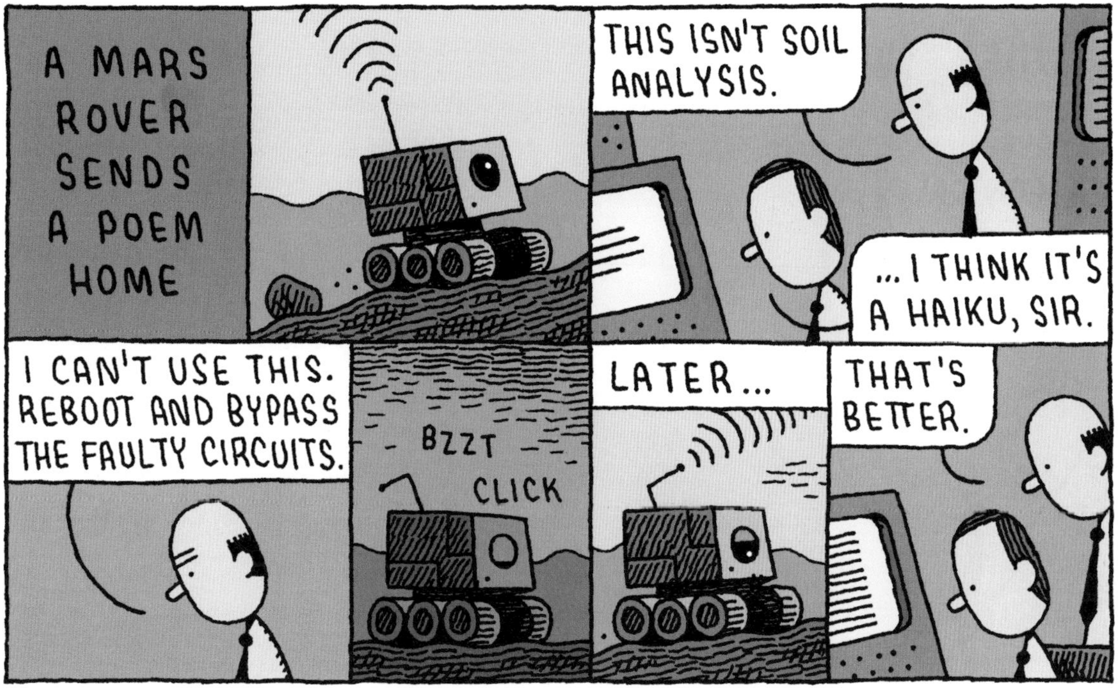
A MARS ROVER SENDS A POEM HOME
THIS ISN'T SOIL ANALYSIS.
... I THINK IT'S A HAIKU, SIR.
I CAN'T USE THIS. REBOOT AND BYPASS THE FAULTY CIRCUITS.
BZZT
CLICK
LATER...
THAT'S BETTER.

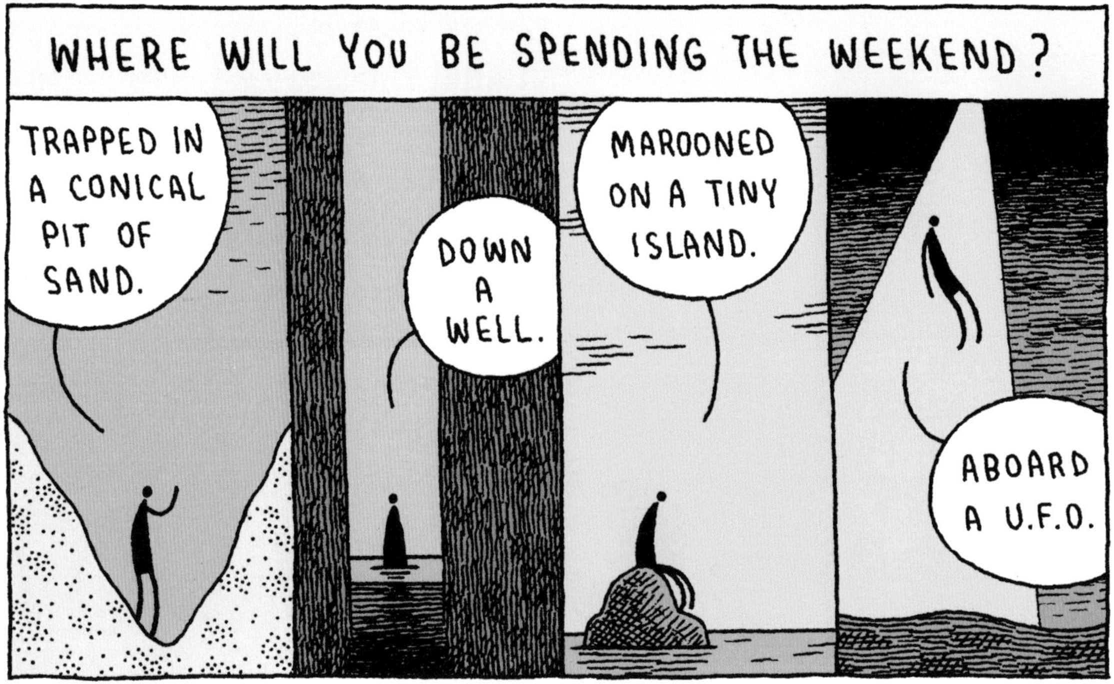
WHERE WILL YOU BE SPENDING THE WEEKEND?
TRAPPED IN A CONICAL PIT OF SAND.
DOWN A WELL.
MAROONED ON A TINY ISLAND.
ABOARD A U.F.O.

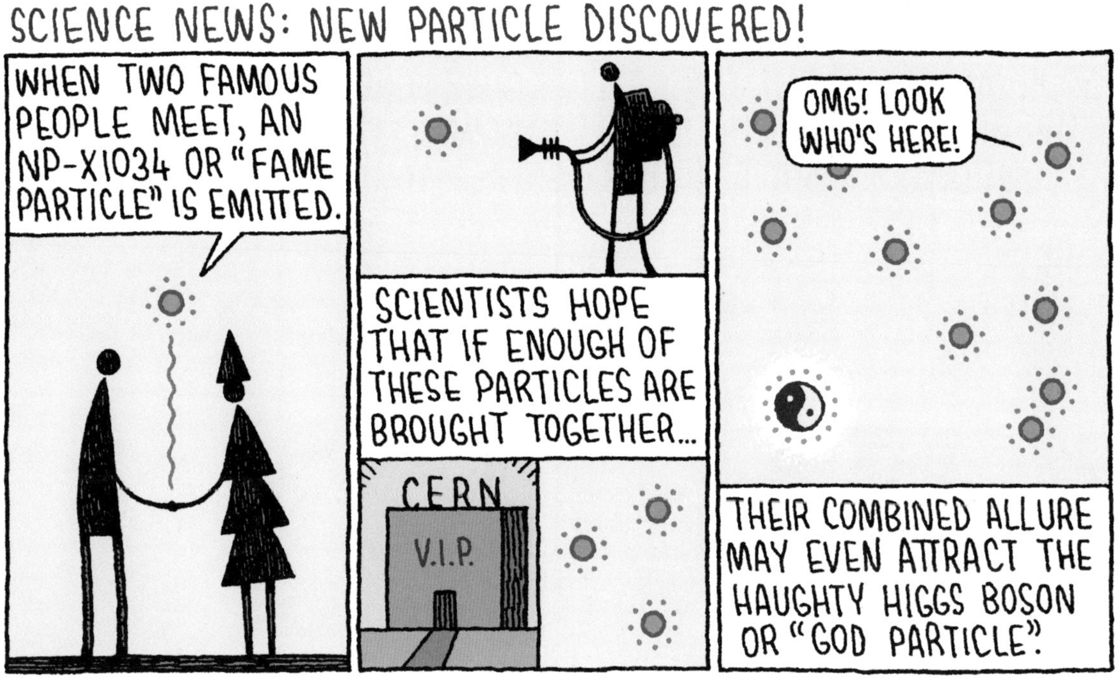
SCIENCE NEWS: NEW PARTICLE DISCOVERED!
WHEN TWO FAMOUS PEOPLE MEET, AN NP-X1034 OR "FAME PARTICLE" IS EMITTED.
SCIENTISTS HOPE THAT IF ENOUGH OF THESE PARTICLES ARE BROUGHT TOGETHER...
CERN
V.I.P.
OMG! LOOK WHO'S HERE!
THEIR COMBINED ALLURE MAY EVEN ATTRACT THE HAUGHTY HIGGS BOSON OR "GOD PARTICLE".

THE COURT OF KING JAMES I, 1611

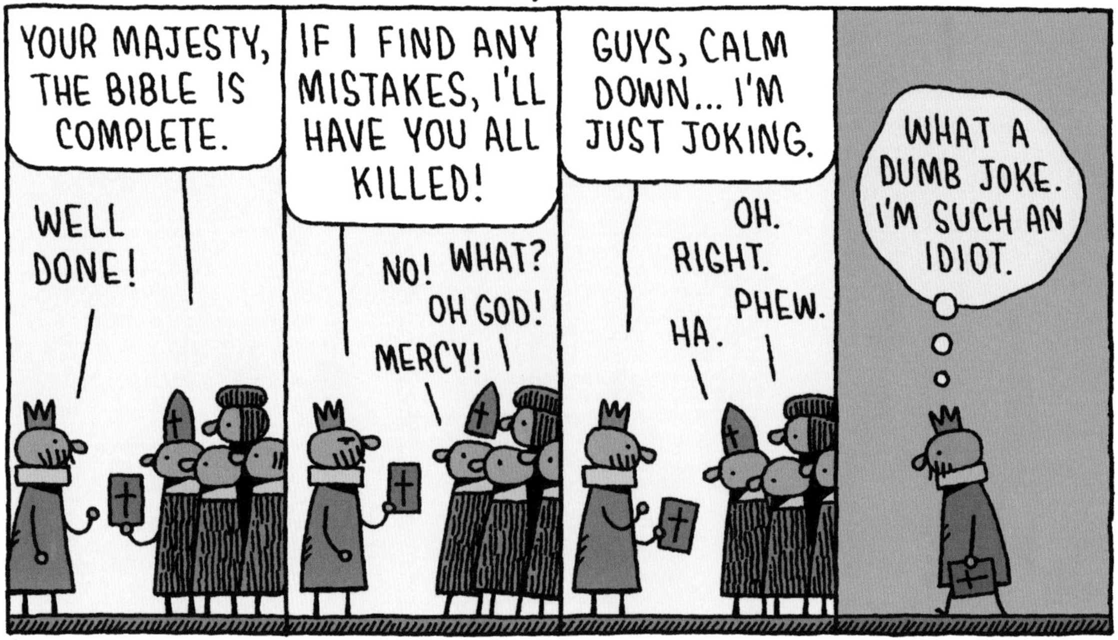
YOUR MAJESTY, THE BIBLE IS COMPLETE.
WELL DONE!
IF I FIND ANY MISTAKES, I'LL HAVE YOU ALL KILLED!
NO!
WHAT?
OH GOD!
MERCY!
GUYS, CALM DOWN... I'M JUST JOKING.
OH. RIGHT.
PHEW.
HA.
WHAT A DUMB JOKE. I'M SUCH AN IDIOT.

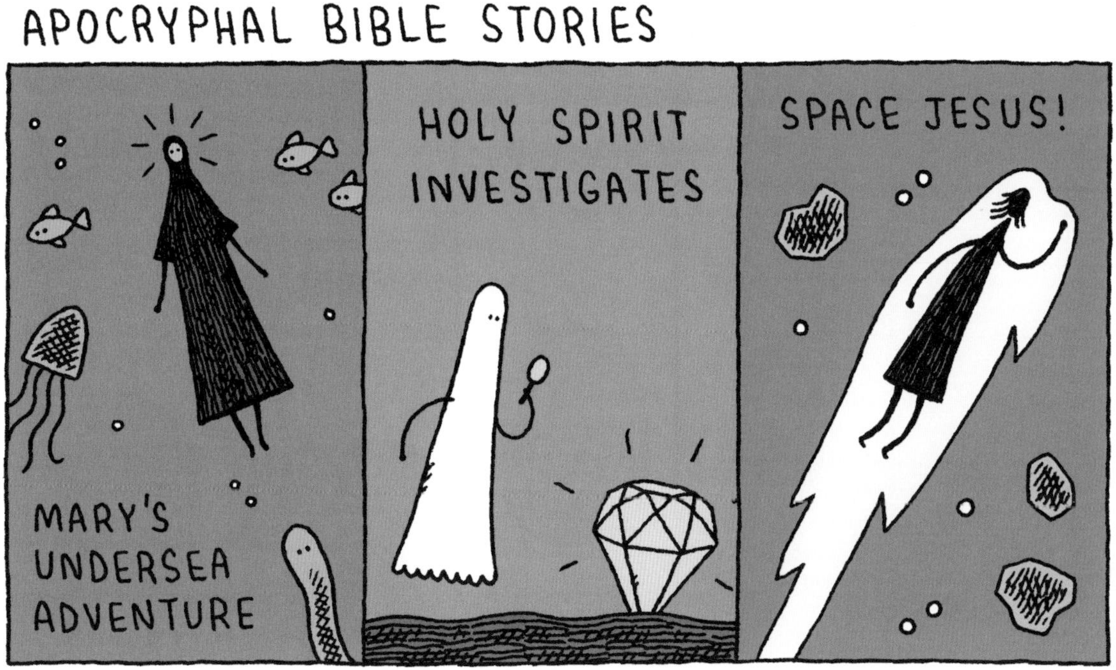
APOCRYPHAL BIBLE STORIES
MARY'S UNDERSEA ADVENTURE
HOLY SPIRIT INVESTIGATES
SPACE JESUS!

WHAT DID YOU WRITE TODAY, MISTER HEMINGWAY?
TALES OF MY MANLY EXPLOITS!
MONDAY
BOOZE-ADDLED NONSENSE.
TUESDAY
A MASTER-PIECE!
WEDNESDAY
NOTHING..
THURSDAY
A SPITEFUL LETTER TO MY WIFE.
FRIDAY

ORDER NOW FOR CHRISTMAS DELIVERY

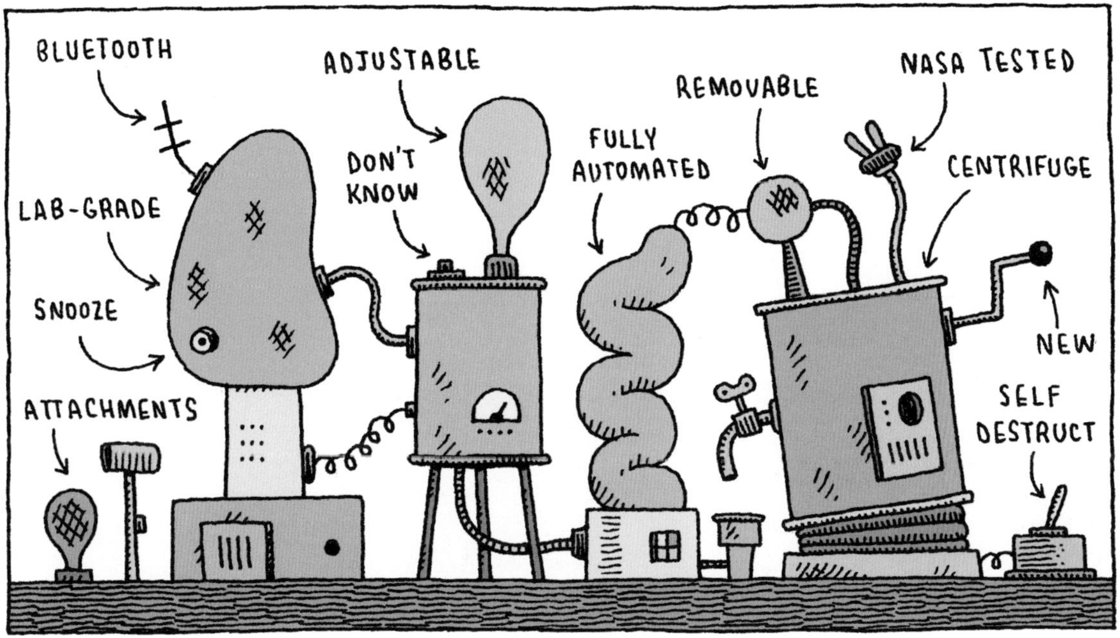
BLUETOOTH
ADJUSTABLE
NASA TESTED
REMOVABLE
FULLY AUTOMATED
DON'T KNOW
CENTRIFUGE
LAB-GRADE
SNOOZE
NEW
SELF DESTRUCT
ATTACHMENTS

1. BŌRUK OREG: CAVEMAN DETECTIVE
2. VICTIM
3. POSSIBLE MURDER WEAPONS
4. TAR PIT
5. FOOTPRINTS
6. PRECIOUS STONE

SOME OF THE ERRORS IN DAN BROWN'S NEW BOOK

THE OVAL OFFICE DOES NOT CONTAIN A "HAUNTED WISHING WELL".

RABBITS ARE MUTE, SO THE PHONE CALL IN CHAPTER THREE IS IMPOSSIBLE.

NASA BROUGHT ROCKS BACK FROM THE MOON, NOT "MYSTERIOUS EGGS".

THE CRAZED AUTHOR CACKLES AS HE PEPPERS HIS PROSE WITH WILLFULLY OBSCURE WORDS.
HA HA
NEVER A THOUGHT FOR HIS INNOCENT VICTIMS!
HE USED WORDS I DIDN'T KNOW!
WHY?
I HAD TO USE A -Sob- DICTIONARY
IT'S A DISGRACE!
CAN NO-ONE RID US OF THIS MENACE?!
HA HA HA

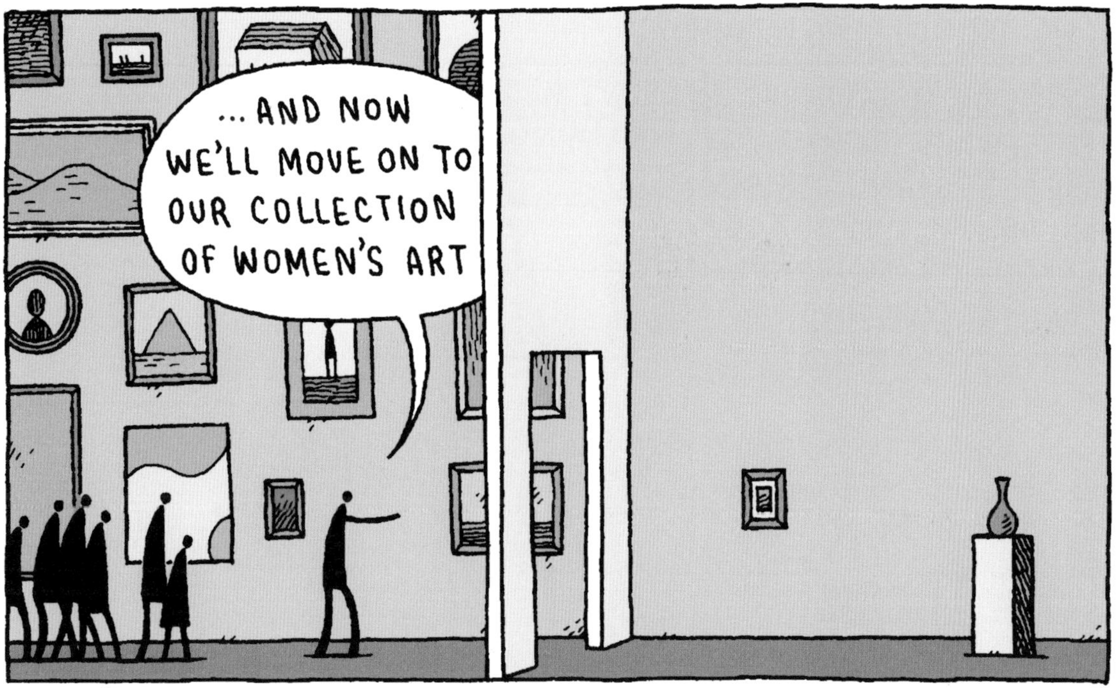
...AND NOW WE'LL MOVE ON TO OUR COLLECTION OF WOMEN'S ART

THE ORIGIN OF SWEARING

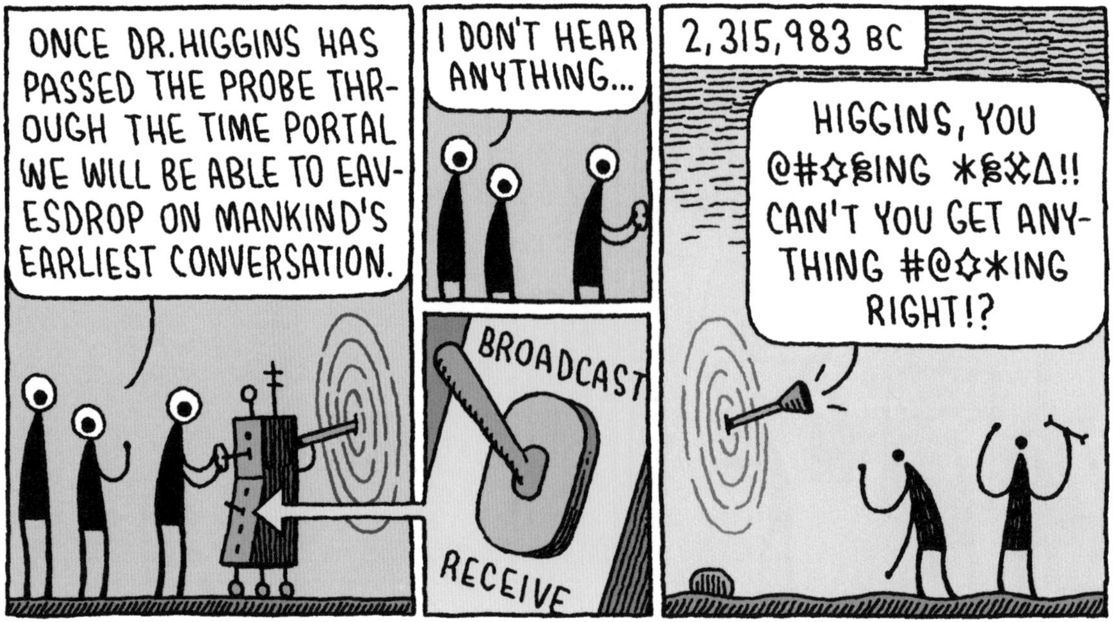
ONCE DR. HIGGINS HAS PASSED THE PROBE THROUGH THE TIME PORTAL WE WILL BE ABLE TO EAVESDROP ON MANKIND'S EARLIEST CONVERSATION.
I DON'T HEAR ANYTHING...
BROADCAST
RECEIVE
2,315,983 BC
HIGGINS, YOU @#✿§ING ✱§✗Δ!! CAN'T YOU GET ANYTHING #@✿✱ING RIGHT!?

THE GIGANTIC SCULPTURE
SWORD (BROKEN)
HEAD (STOLEN)
ARMS (LOST)
HORSE (MELTED DOWN)
FEET (KNOCKED OFF)

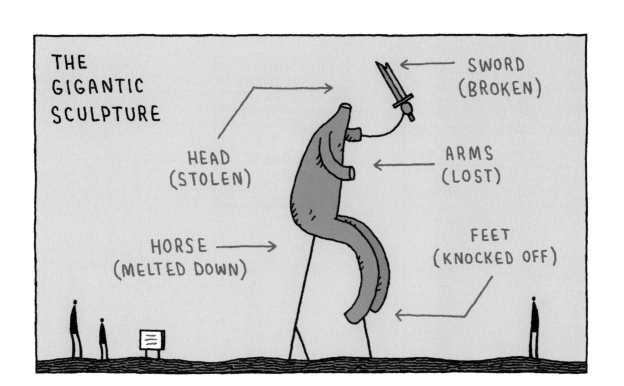

SOUTH BANK, LONDON, 1950

OH BOY! I'M SO PROUD TO BE PART OF THE FESTIVAL OF BRITAIN! WHAT LUCK THAT I'M HERE: RIGHT AT THE CENTRE OF IT ALL!

WHAT'S <u>THAT</u> STILL DOING HERE?

DON'T WORRY, THE REPLACEMENT ARRIVES TOMORROW.

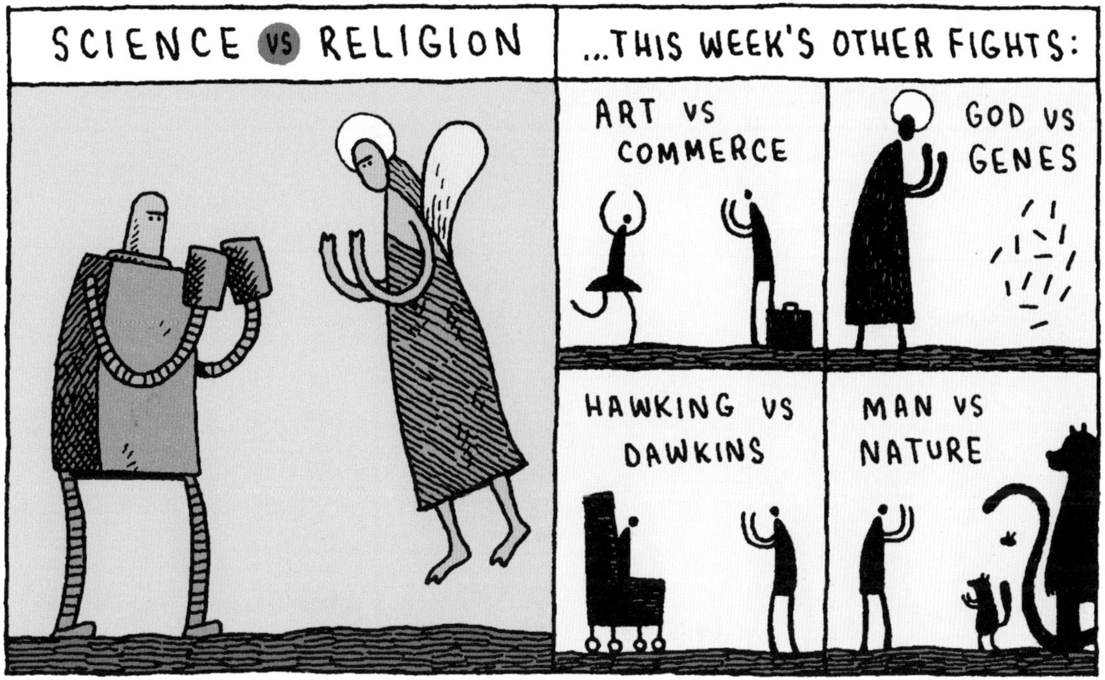
SCIENCE VS RELIGION
...THIS WEEK'S OTHER FIGHTS:
ART VS COMMERCE
GOD VS GENES
HAWKING VS DAWKINS
MAN VS NATURE

INNOVATIONS AT THE BRITISH LIBRARY

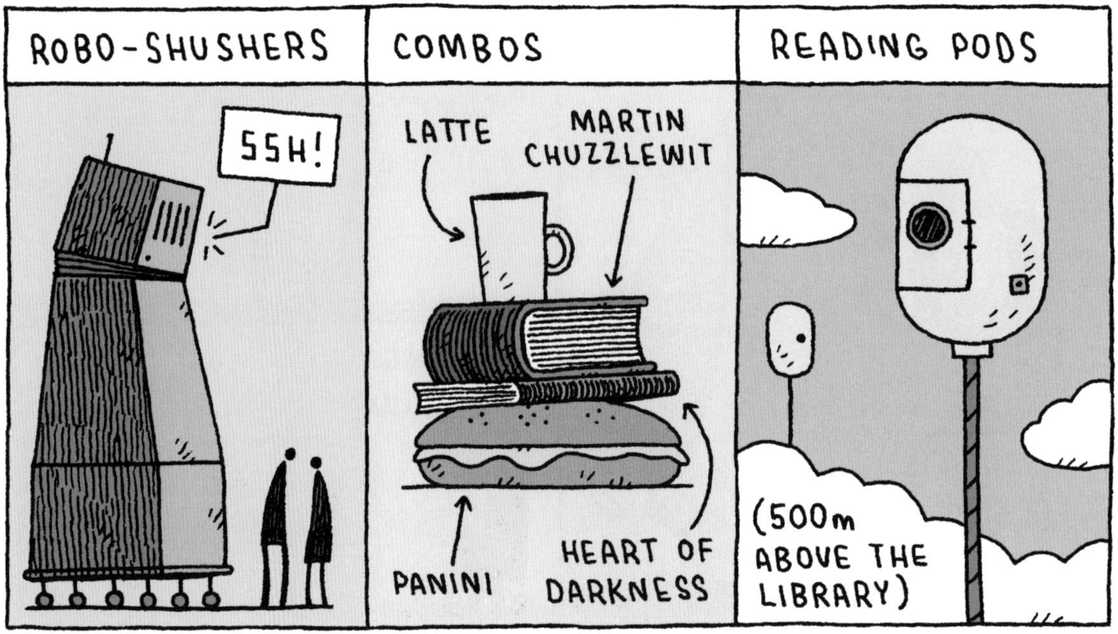

ROBO-SHUSHERS
SSH!
COMBOS
LATTE
MARTIN CHUZZLEWIT
PANINI
HEART OF DARKNESS
READING PODS
(500m ABOVE THE LIBRARY)

GUIDE THE METROPOLITAN INTELLECTUAL BACK TO HIS IVORY TOWER WITHOUT ENCOUNTERING HIS COUNTRYMEN

THE FAMILY OF WRITERS

THE SAINTLY MOTHER WITH AN UNGRATEFUL FAMILY: A MEMOIR

I WISH I WAS A PRINCESS: A TALE OF REGRET

THE DEAD CAT: A MYSTERY

THE STUPID DOG: A NOVEL

IDIOT: A BIOGRAPHY OF MY FATHER

LAZY: THE STORY OF TODAY'S PAMPERED YOUTH

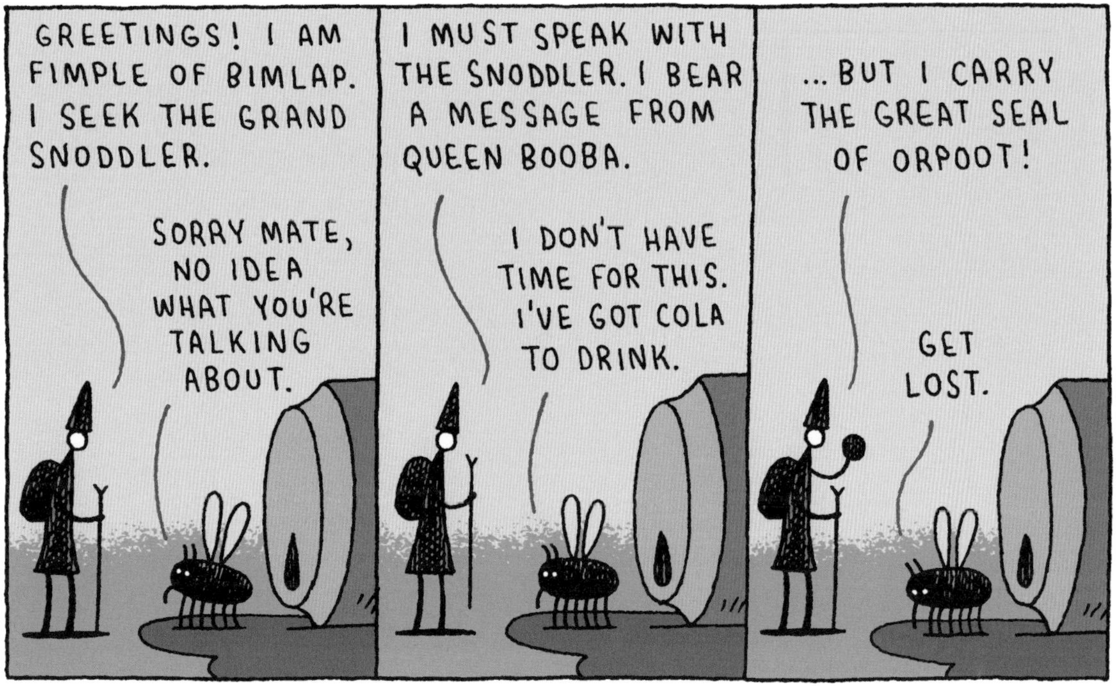
GREETINGS! I AM FIMPLE OF BIMLAP. I SEEK THE GRAND SNODDLER.
SORRY MATE, NO IDEA WHAT YOU'RE TALKING ABOUT.
I MUST SPEAK WITH THE SNODDLER. I BEAR A MESSAGE FROM QUEEN BOOBA.
I DON'T HAVE TIME FOR THIS. I'VE GOT COLA TO DRINK.
...BUT I CARRY THE GREAT SEAL OF ORPOOT!
GET LOST.

Mister Victorian Novel
UGH. HERE COMES MISTER VICTORIAN PAINTING. HOW I DESPISE HIM!
GOOD DAY TO YOU, SIR.
AND TO YOU.
PRETENTIOUS WINDBAG.
VULGAR SIMPLETON.

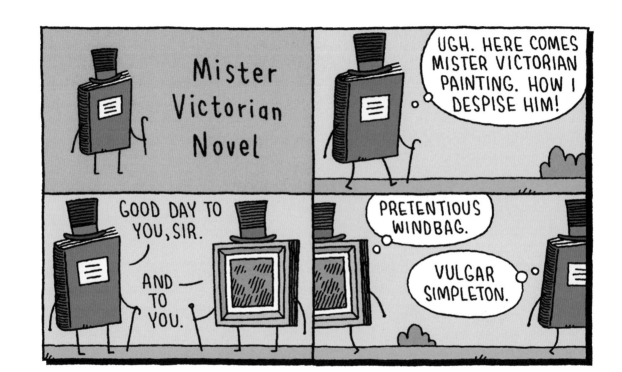

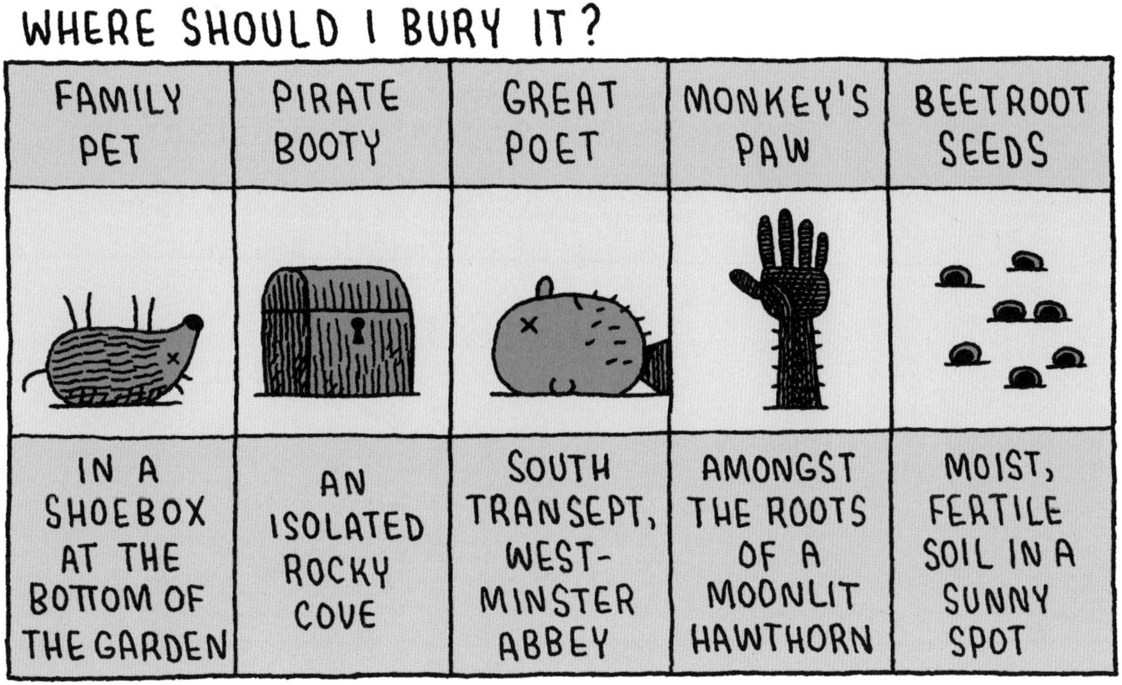
WHERE SHOULD I BURY IT?
FAMILY PET
IN A SHOEBOX AT THE BOTTOM OF THE GARDEN
PIRATE BOOTY
AN ISOLATED ROCKY COVE
GREAT POET
SOUTH TRANSEPT, WEST-MINSTER ABBEY
MONKEY'S PAW
AMONGST THE ROOTS OF A MOONLIT HAWTHORN
BEETROOT SEEDS
MOIST, FERTILE SOIL IN A SUNNY SPOT

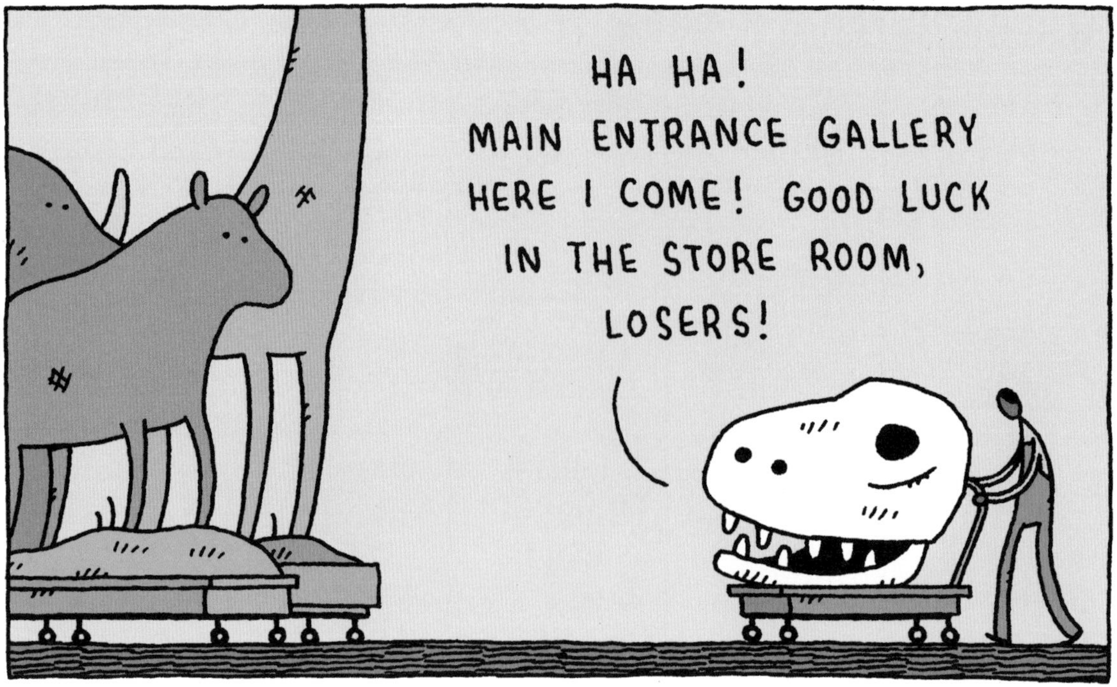
HA HA!
MAIN ENTRANCE GALLERY HERE I COME! GOOD LUCK IN THE STORE ROOM, LOSERS!

READER OFFER! Holiday in a futuristic dystopia

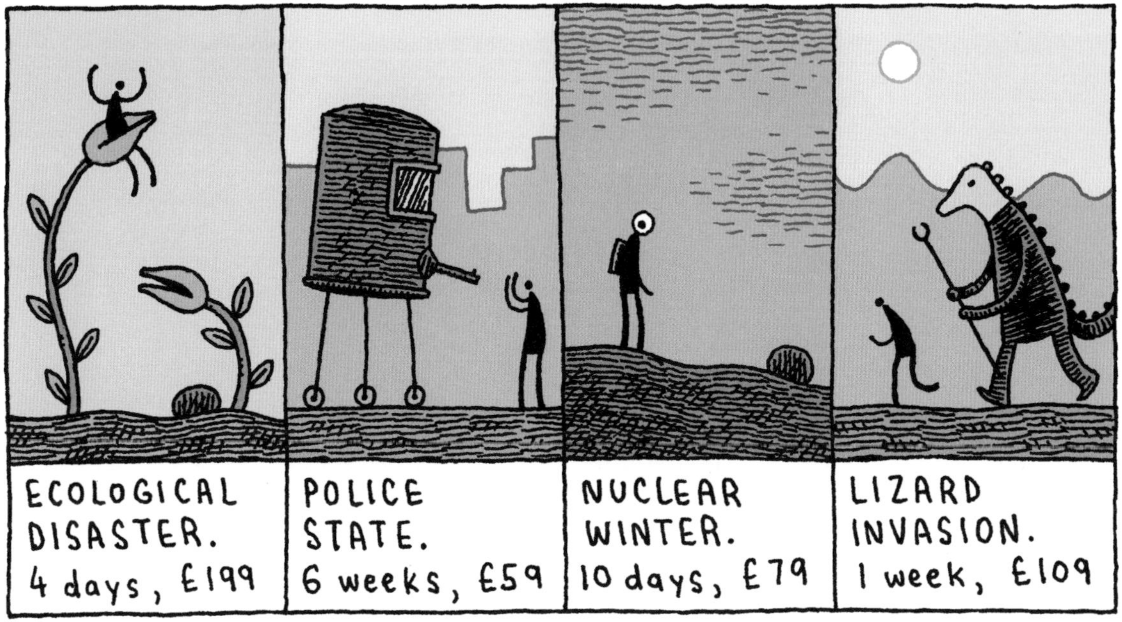
ECOLOGICAL DISASTER.
4 days, £199
POLICE STATE.
6 weeks, £59
NUCLEAR WINTER.
10 days, £79
LIZARD INVASION.
1 week, £109

NOCTURNAL GOINGS ON IN THE SALTMARSHES

THE SPY SIGNALS TO A ZEPPELIN

THE SMUGGLERS GO ABOUT THEIR BUSINESS

THE TERRIFYING BEAST PROWLS

THE SECRET LOVERS CANOODLE

THERE ARE FIVE ERRORS IN THIS CARTOON ABOUT MARTIN AMIS, CAN YOU SPOT THEM ALL?

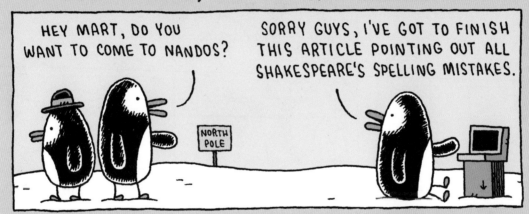

HEY MART, DO YOU WANT TO COME TO NANDOS?

SORRY GUYS, I'VE GOT TO FINISH THIS ARTICLE POINTING OUT ALL SHAKESPEARE'S SPELLING MISTAKES.

NORTH POLE

ERRORS: 1. PENGUINS LIVE AT THE SOUTH POLE 2. POSSESSIVE APOSTROPHE MISSING IN 'NANDO'S', 3. MARTIN AMIS IS NOT A PENGUIN 4. THE LAPTOP IS NOT SWITCHED ON 5. ONE OF THE PENGUINS IS WEARING A TRILBY.

THE GREAT ARTISTS' COLLABORATION
A MEETING OF MINDS!
THE CREATIVE PROCESS!
SUCCESS!

SOME OF THE SYMBOLS IN MY EPIC NOVEL
WEATHERED STATUE
LOST BALLOON
BROKEN SUNDIAL
ESCAPED CANARY ON GRAVESTONE
SINGLE WINTER BLOOM
DETACHED BICYCLE WHEEL
ROTTEN TREESTUMP

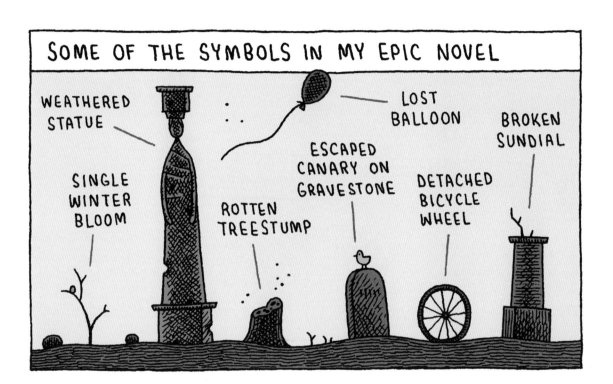

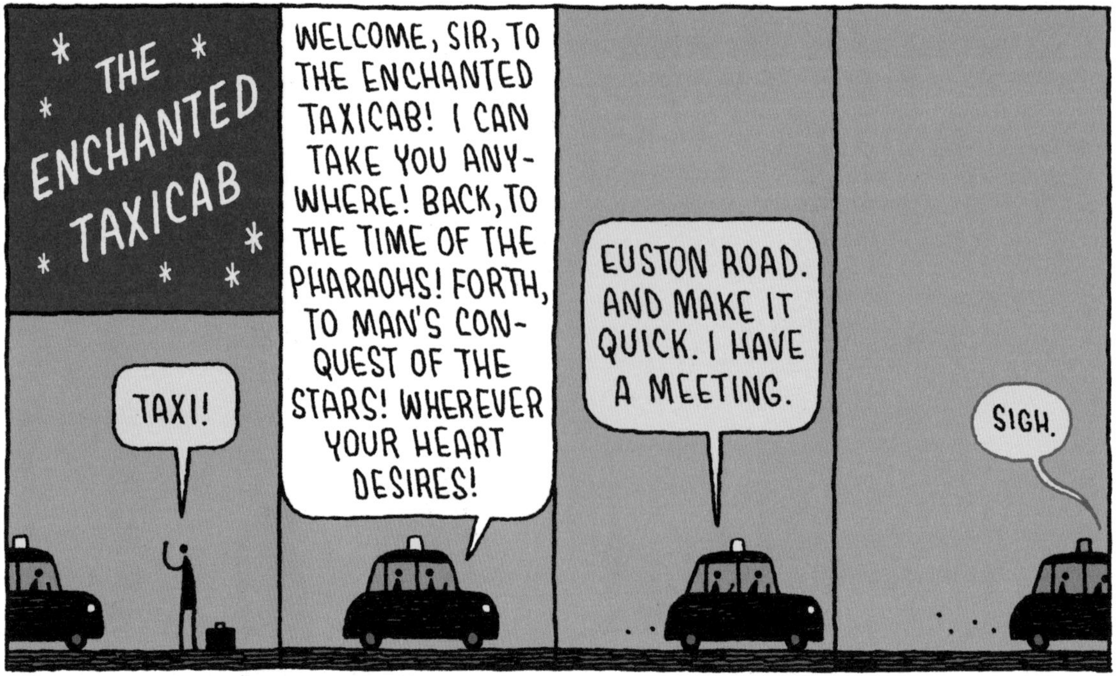
THE ENCHANTED TAXICAB
TAXI!
WELCOME, SIR, TO THE ENCHANTED TAXICAB! I CAN TAKE YOU ANY-WHERE! BACK, TO THE TIME OF THE PHARAOHS! FORTH, TO MAN'S CON-QUEST OF THE STARS! WHEREVER YOUR HEART DESIRES!
EUSTON ROAD. AND MAKE IT QUICK. I HAVE A MEETING.
SIGH.

AWAITING OUR NEW PRIME MINISTER ON HIS DESK

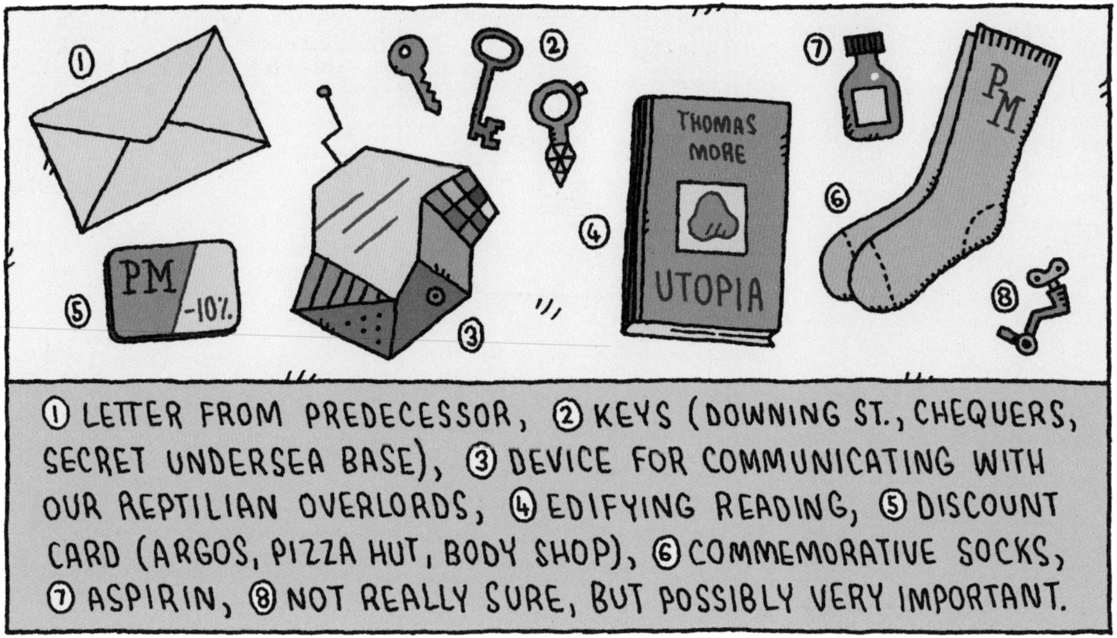
THOMAS MORE
UTOPIA
PM
-10%
PM
① LETTER FROM PREDECESSOR, ② KEYS (DOWNING ST., CHEQUERS, SECRET UNDERSEA BASE), ③ DEVICE FOR COMMUNICATING WITH OUR REPTILIAN OVERLORDS, ④ EDIFYING READING, ⑤ DISCOUNT CARD (ARGOS, PIZZA HUT, BODY SHOP), ⑥ COMMEMORATIVE SOCKS, ⑦ ASPIRIN, ⑧ NOT REALLY SURE, BUT POSSIBLY VERY IMPORTANT.

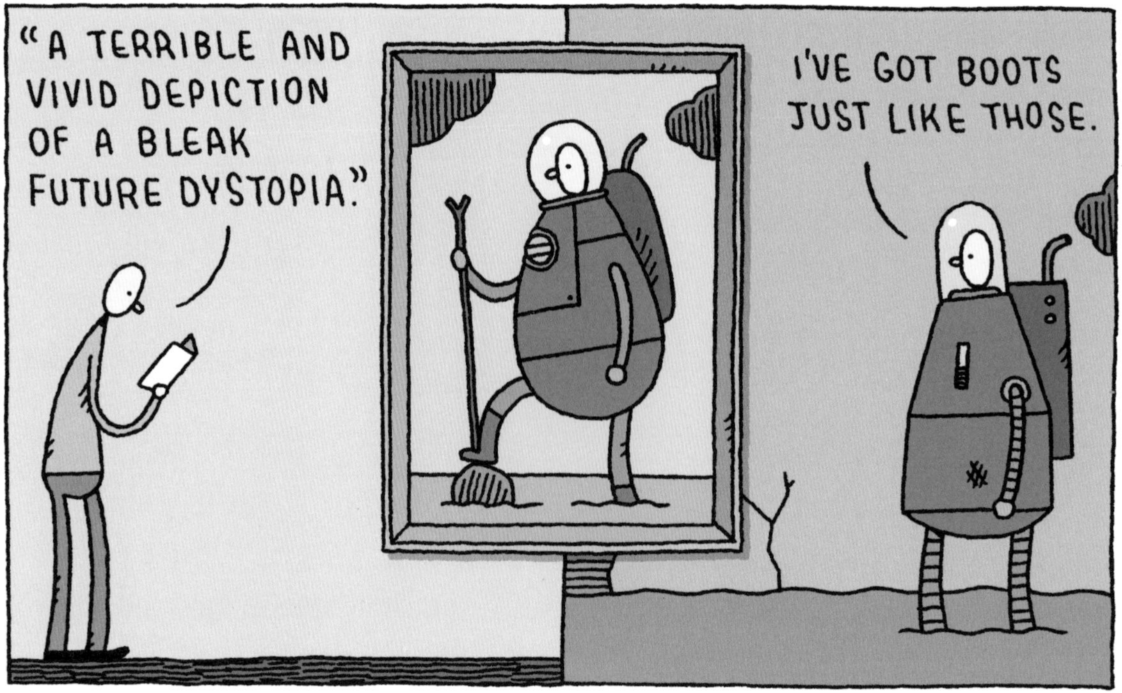
"A TERRIBLE AND VIVID DEPICTION OF A BLEAK FUTURE DYSTOPIA."
I'VE GOT BOOTS JUST LIKE THOSE.

THE REALIST NOVEL AND THE EXPERIMENTAL NOVEL

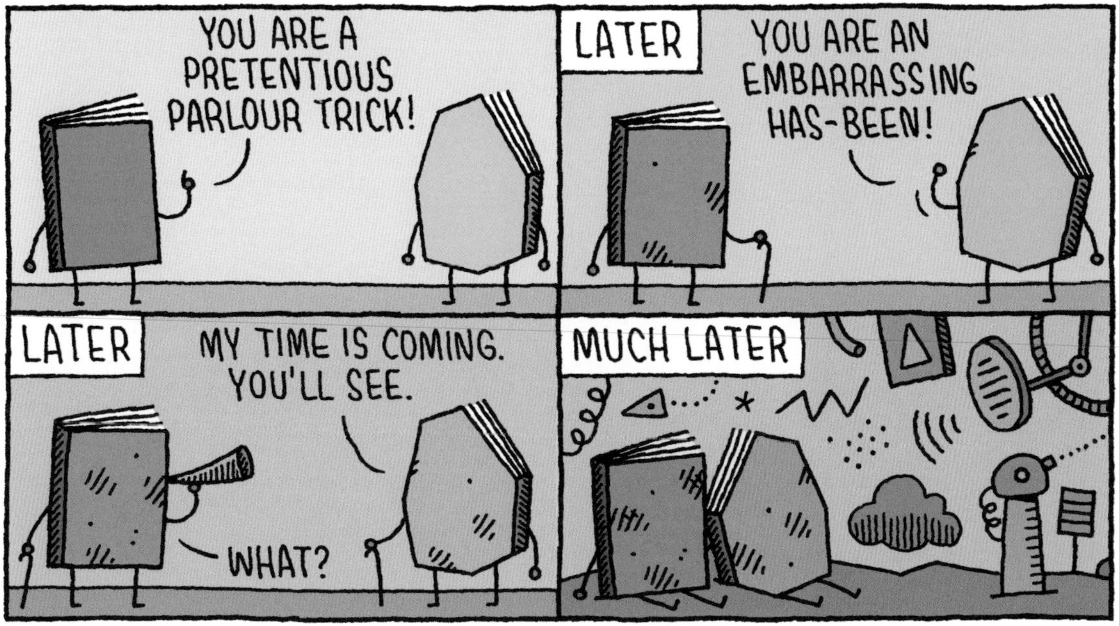

YOU ARE A PRETENTIOUS PARLOUR TRICK!
LATER
YOU ARE AN EMBARRASSING HAS-BEEN!
LATER
MY TIME IS COMING. YOU'LL SEE.
WHAT?
MUCH LATER

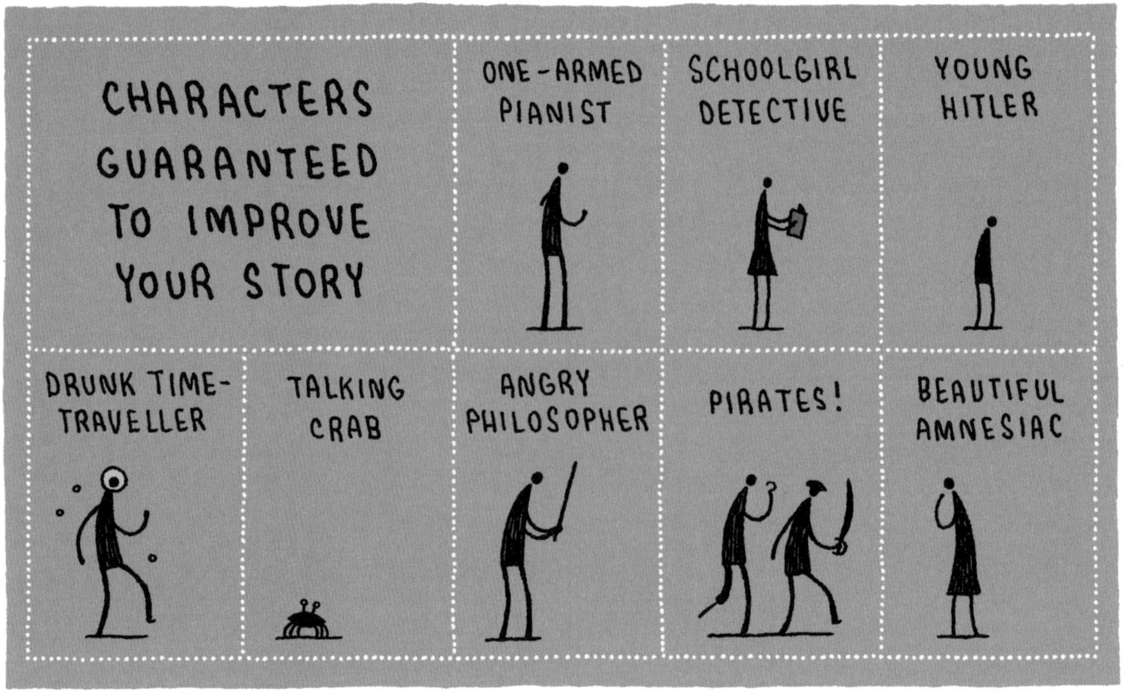
CHARACTERS GUARANTEED TO IMPROVE YOUR STORY
ONE-ARMED PIANIST
SCHOOLGIRL DETECTIVE
YOUNG HITLER
DRUNK TIME-TRAVELLER
TALKING CRAB
ANGRY PHILOSOPHER
PIRATES!
BEAUTIFUL AMNESIAC

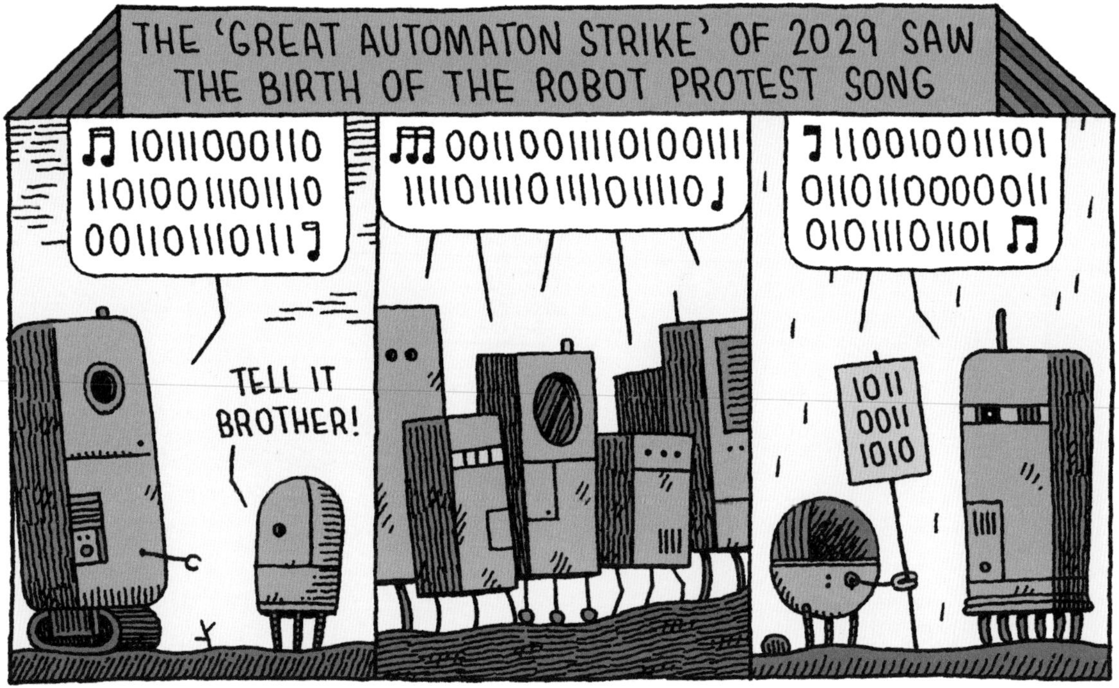
THE 'GREAT AUTOMATON STRIKE' OF 2029 SAW THE BIRTH OF THE ROBOT PROTEST SONG
♫ 10111000110 11010011101110 0011011101111 ♪
TELL IT BROTHER!
♫ 00110011110100111 11110111101111011110 ♩
♪ 110010011101 0110110000011 01011101101 ♫
1011 0011 1010

LA TRAVIATA

ACT I, SCENE 2. VIOLETTA IS BANISHED FROM THE PALACE FOR BREAKING THE ENCHANTED TEACUP.

ACT II, SCENE 1. HUMBERT (DISGUISED AS A ROCK) WOOS VIOLETTA WITH A MOONLIGHT SERENADE.

ACT III, SCENE 3. VIOLETTA, HUMBERT, BOBO AND THE BARON ARE KILLED. THE INSECT KING SINGS A FINAL LAMENT.

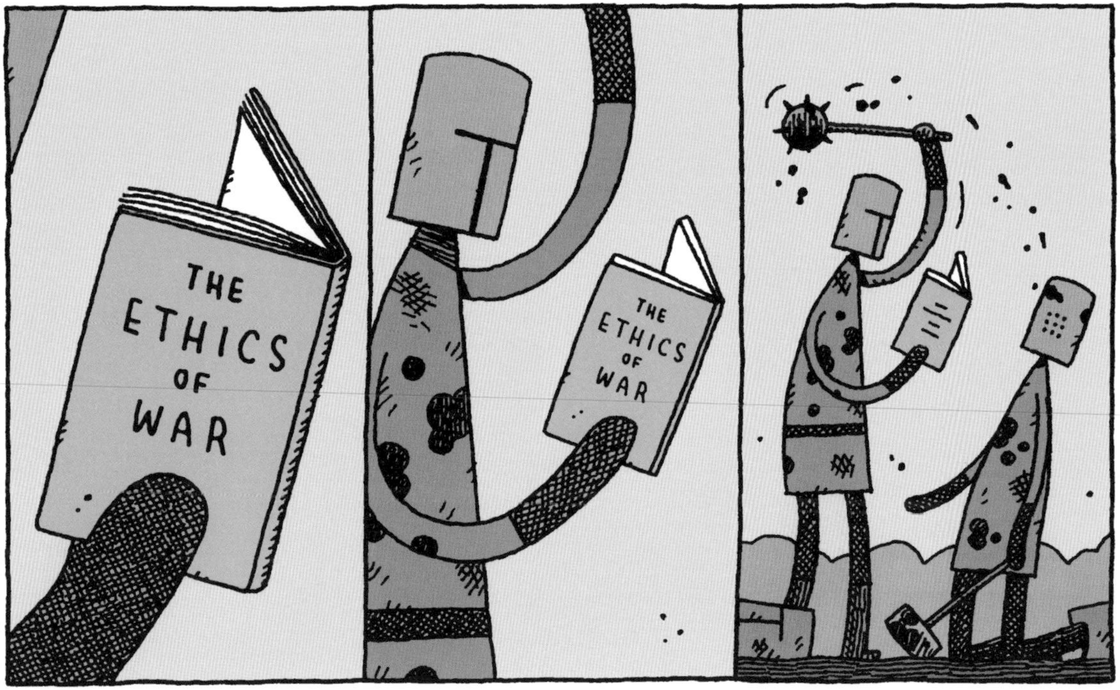
THE ETHICS OF WAR
THE ETHICS OF WAR

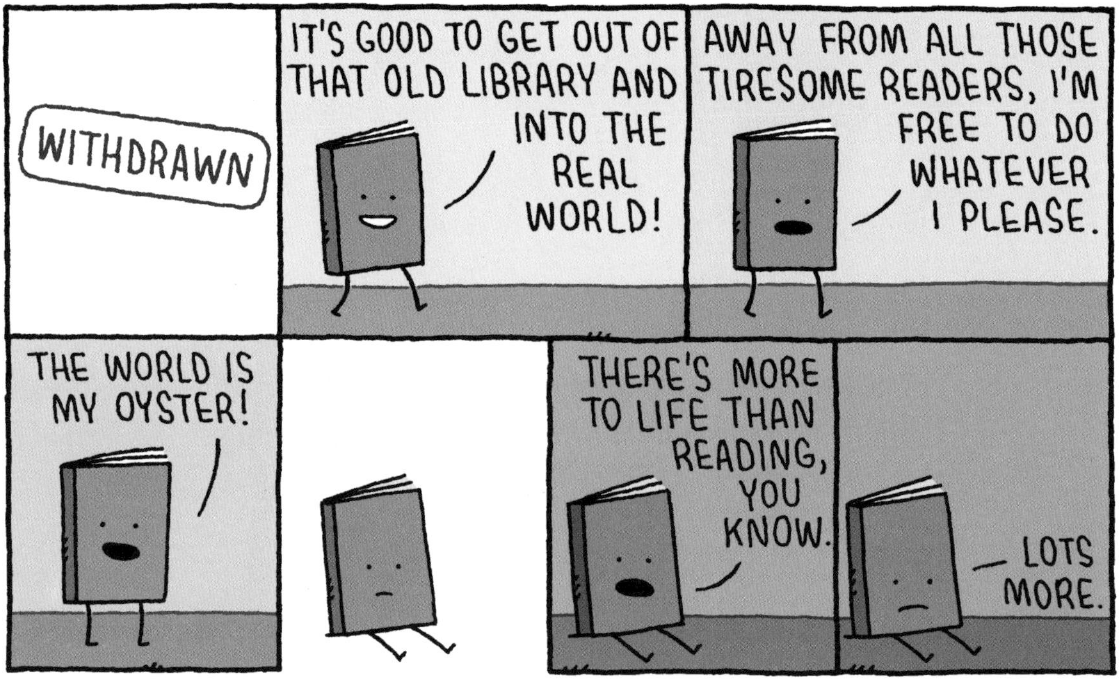
WITHDRAWN
IT'S GOOD TO GET OUT OF THAT OLD LIBRARY AND INTO THE REAL WORLD!
AWAY FROM ALL THOSE TIRESOME READERS, I'M FREE TO DO WHATEVER I PLEASE.
THE WORLD IS MY OYSTER!
THERE'S MORE TO LIFE THAN READING, YOU KNOW.
LOTS MORE.

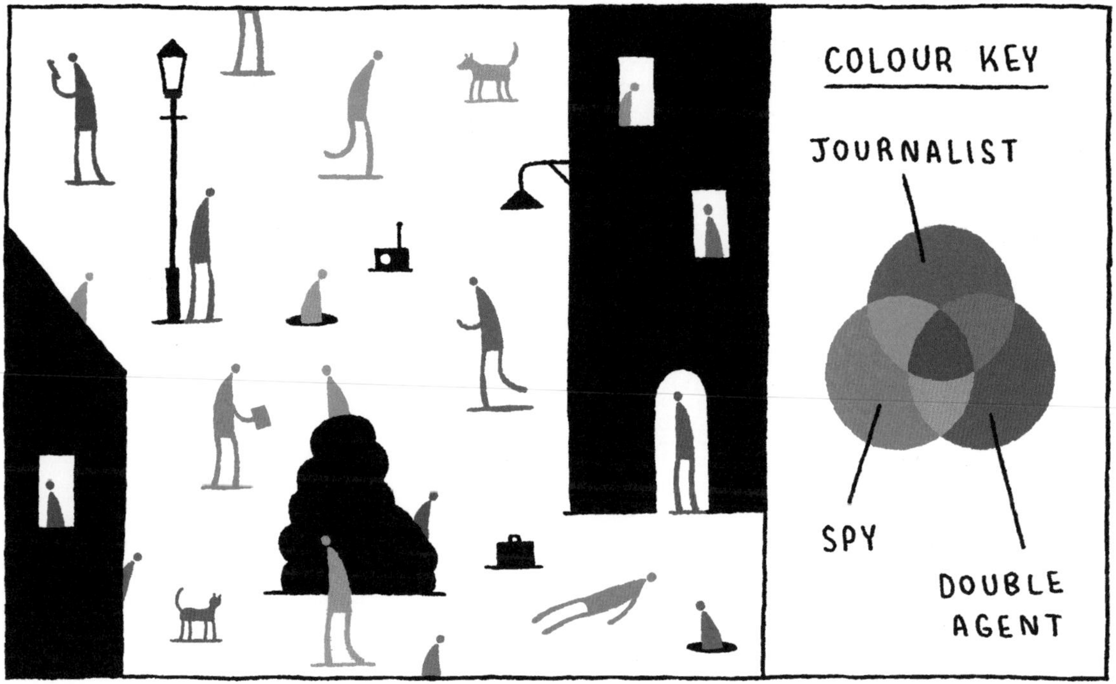
COLOUR KEY
JOURNALIST
SPY
DOUBLE AGENT

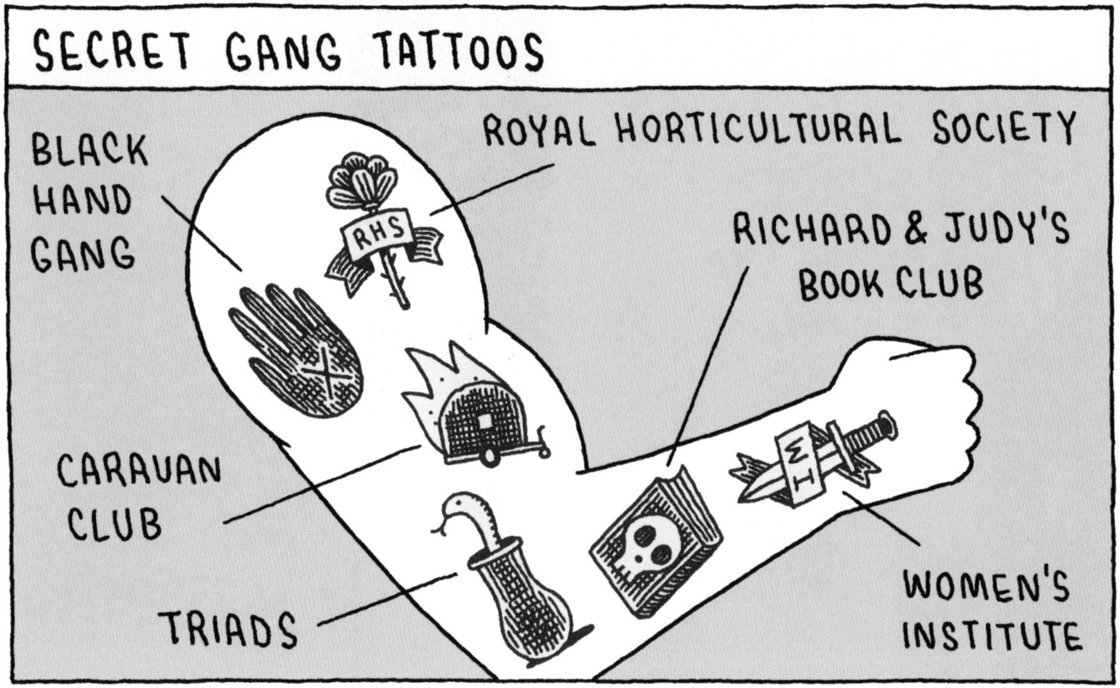
SECRET GANG TATTOOS
BLACK HAND GANG
ROYAL HORTICULTURAL SOCIETY
RHS
RICHARD & JUDY'S BOOK CLUB
CARAVAN CLUB
WI
TRIADS
WOMEN'S INSTITUTE

A METAPHORICAL CARTOON
WHAT IS THIS NONSENSE?
I THINK YOU REPRESENT WESTERN SOCIETY.
AND YOU?
"THE BIRD OF HOPE ATOP THE PINEAPPLE OF HISTORY."
AND ME?
I'M PRETTY SURE YOU DON'T MEAN ANYTHING. YOU'RE JUST A WORM.
Sob!

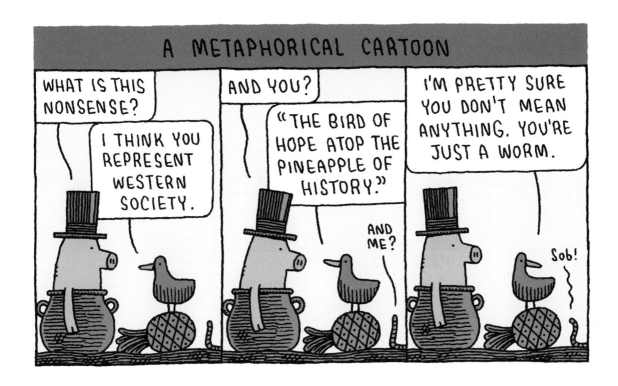

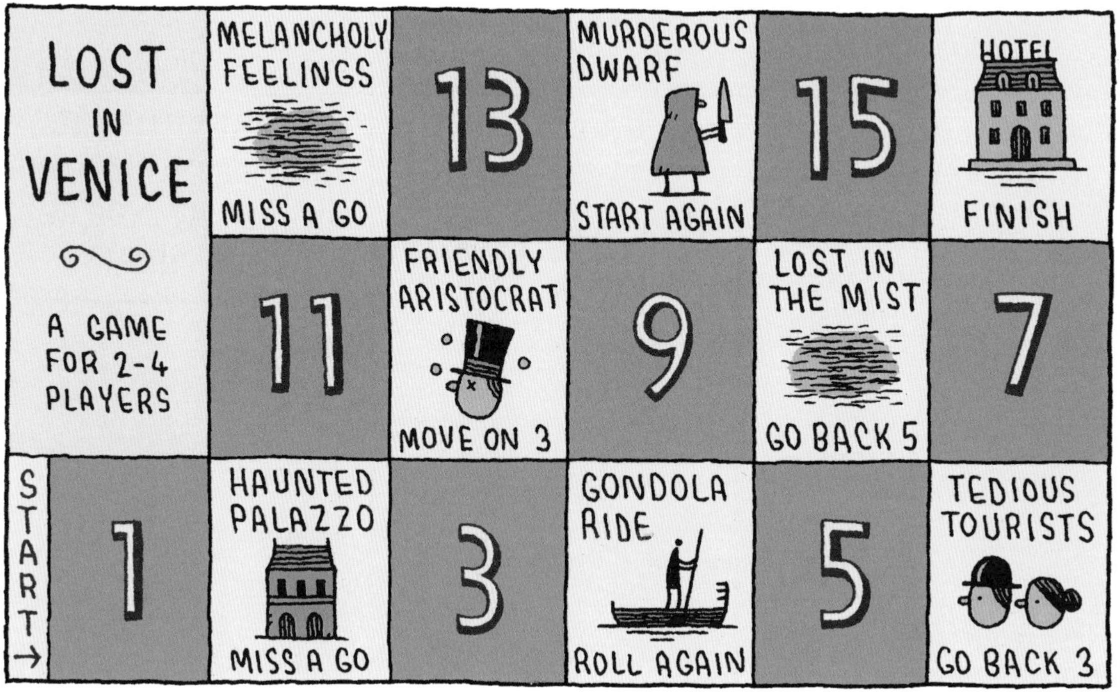
LOST IN VENICE
A GAME FOR 2-4 PLAYERS
START
1
HAUNTED PALAZZO
MISS A GO
3
GONDOLA RIDE
ROLL AGAIN
5
TEDIOUS TOURISTS
GO BACK 3
7
LOST IN THE MIST
GO BACK 5
9
FRIENDLY ARISTOCRAT
MOVE ON 3
11
MELANCHOLY FEELINGS
MISS A GO
13
MURDEROUS DWARF
START AGAIN
15
HOTEL
FINISH

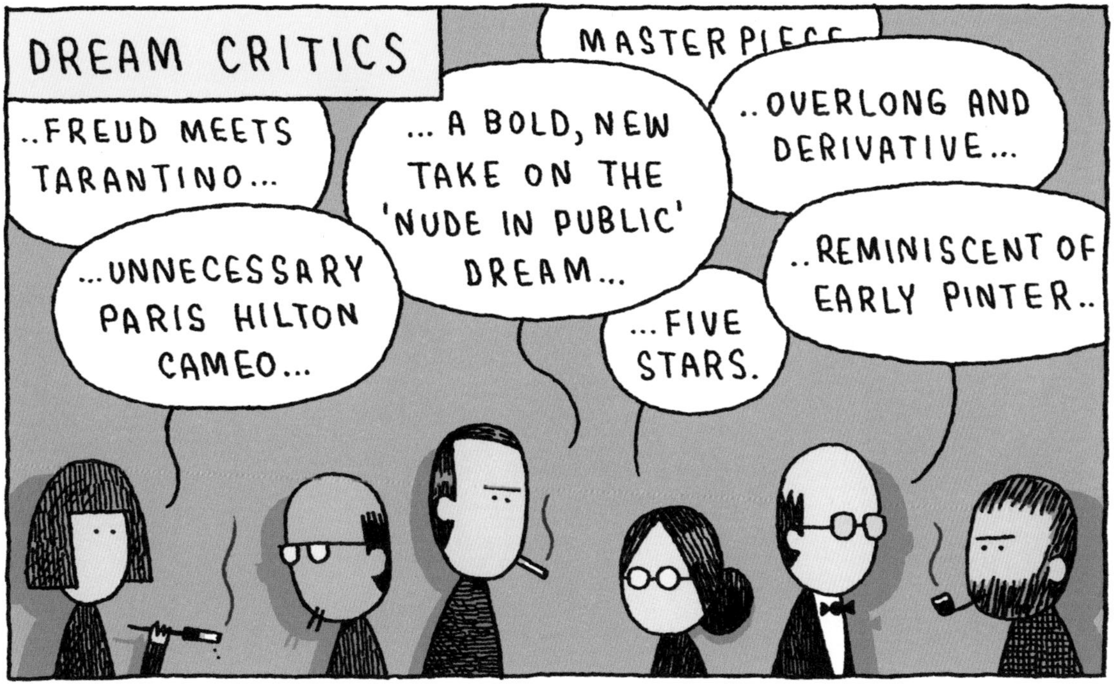
DREAM CRITICS
MASTERPI
..FREUD MEETS TARANTINO...
... A BOLD, NEW TAKE ON THE 'NUDE IN PUBLIC' DREAM...
..OVERLONG AND DERIVATIVE...
...UNNECESSARY PARIS HILTON CAMEO...
...FIVE STARS.
..REMINISCENT OF EARLY PINTER..

FROM THE RUINS OF CIVILISATION, ONE GROUP ROSE UP AND SEIZED POWER.

THE TIME OF THE MORRIS MEN HAD BEGUN...

INSPECTOR GOD: OMNISCIENT DETECTIVE

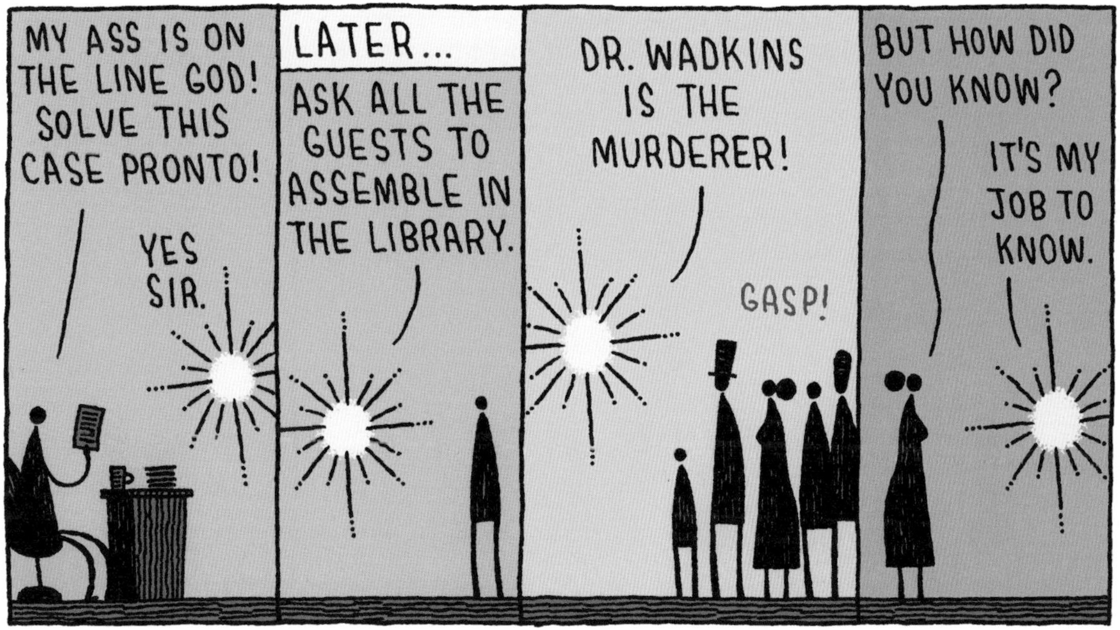

MY ASS IS ON THE LINE GOD! SOLVE THIS CASE PRONTO!
YES SIR.
LATER...
ASK ALL THE GUESTS TO ASSEMBLE IN THE LIBRARY.
DR. WADKINS IS THE MURDERER!
GASP!
BUT HOW DID YOU KNOW?
IT'S MY JOB TO KNOW.

AN ANT REMEMBERS THE MAKING OF 'UN CHIEN ANDALOU'

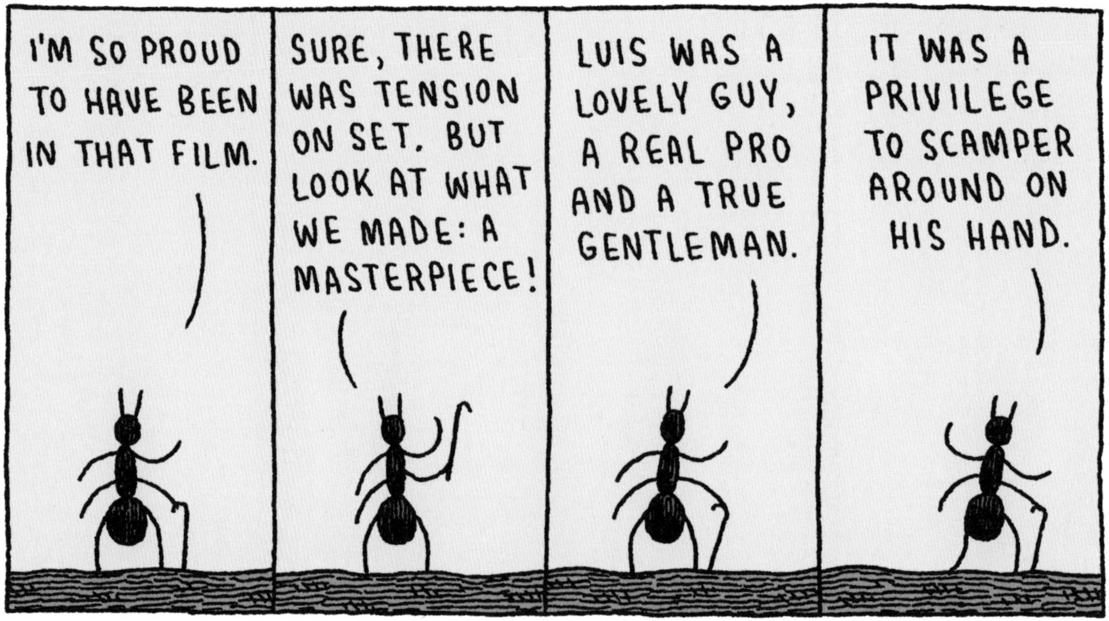

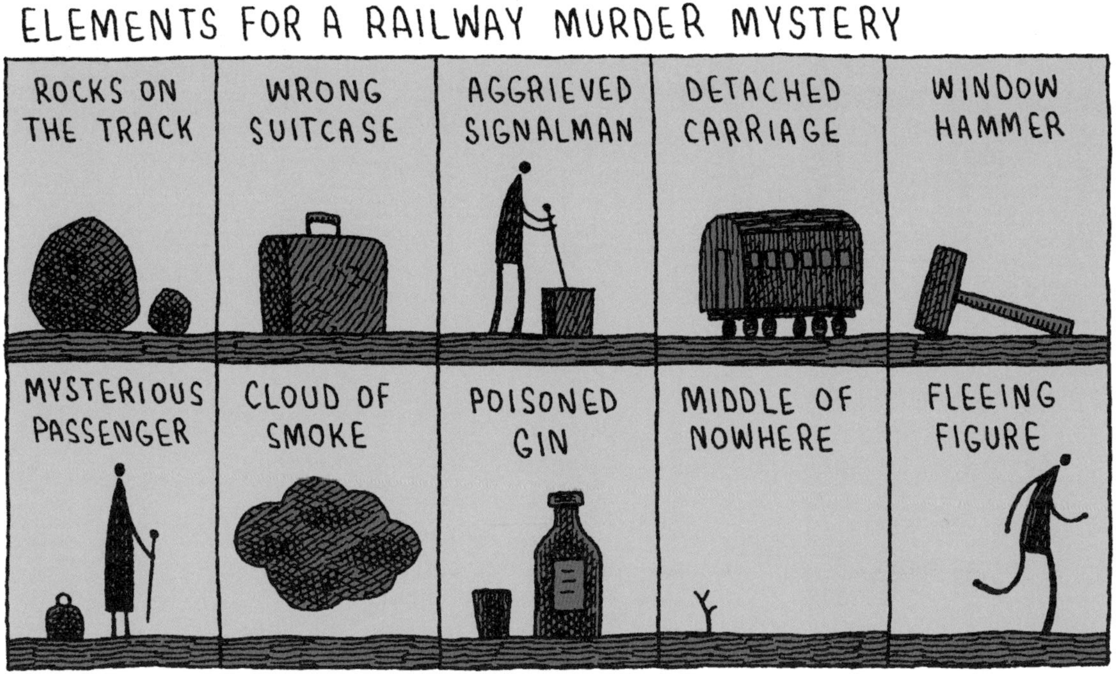
ELEMENTS FOR A RAILWAY MURDER MYSTERY
ROCKS ON THE TRACK
WRONG SUITCASE
AGGRIEVED SIGNALMAN
DETACHED CARRIAGE
WINDOW HAMMER
MYSTERIOUS PASSENGER
CLOUD OF SMOKE
POISONED GIN
MIDDLE OF NOWHERE
FLEEING FIGURE

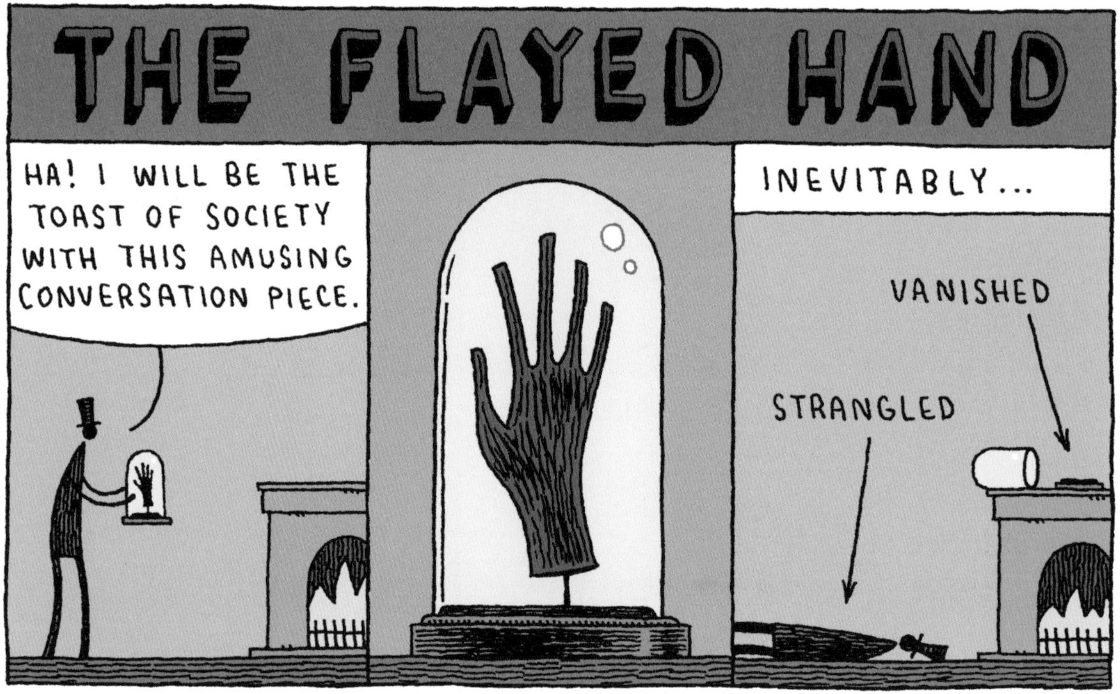
THE FLAYED HAND
HA! I WILL BE THE TOAST OF SOCIETY WITH THIS AMUSING CONVERSATION PIECE.
INEVITABLY...
VANISHED
STRANGLED

BOOK COVER DESIGN IS EASY
ROMANCE
HORROR
COOKERY
THRILLER
HISTORY
SCI-FI
D.I.Y.
NEW AGE

tap
tap tap
taptap ta
tap
ap

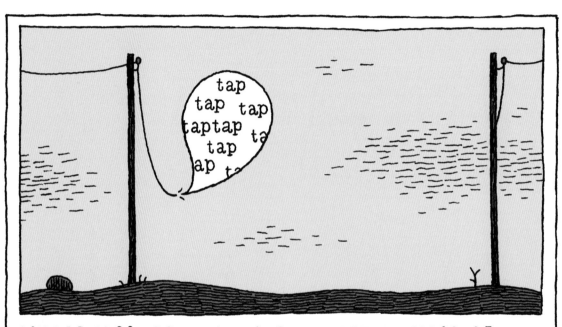

WILDERNESS. BROKEN CABLE. IMPORTANT MESSAGE.

2016: THE 'AGE-APPROPRIATE MUSIC' ACT COMES INTO FORCE

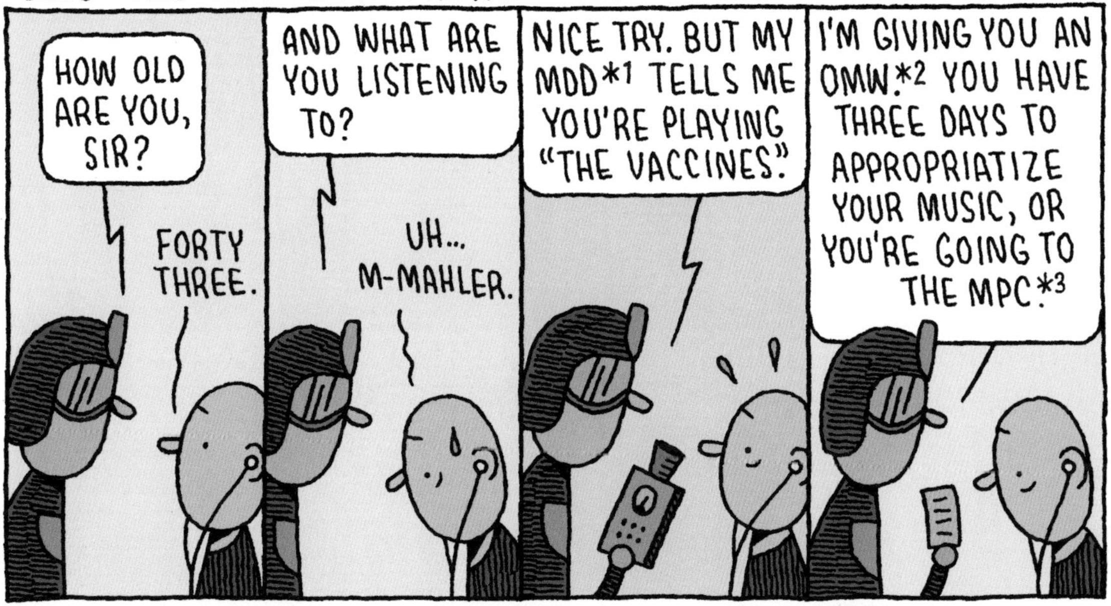

HOW OLD ARE YOU, SIR?
FORTY THREE.
AND WHAT ARE YOU LISTENING TO?
UH... M-MAHLER.
NICE TRY. BUT MY MDD*1 TELLS ME YOU'RE PLAYING "THE VACCINES."
I'M GIVING YOU AN OMW.*2 YOU HAVE THREE DAYS TO APPROPRIATIZE YOUR MUSIC, OR YOU'RE GOING TO THE MPC.*3

*1: MUSIC DETECTION DEVICE *2: OFFICIAL MUSIC WARNING *3: MARTIAN PENAL COLONY

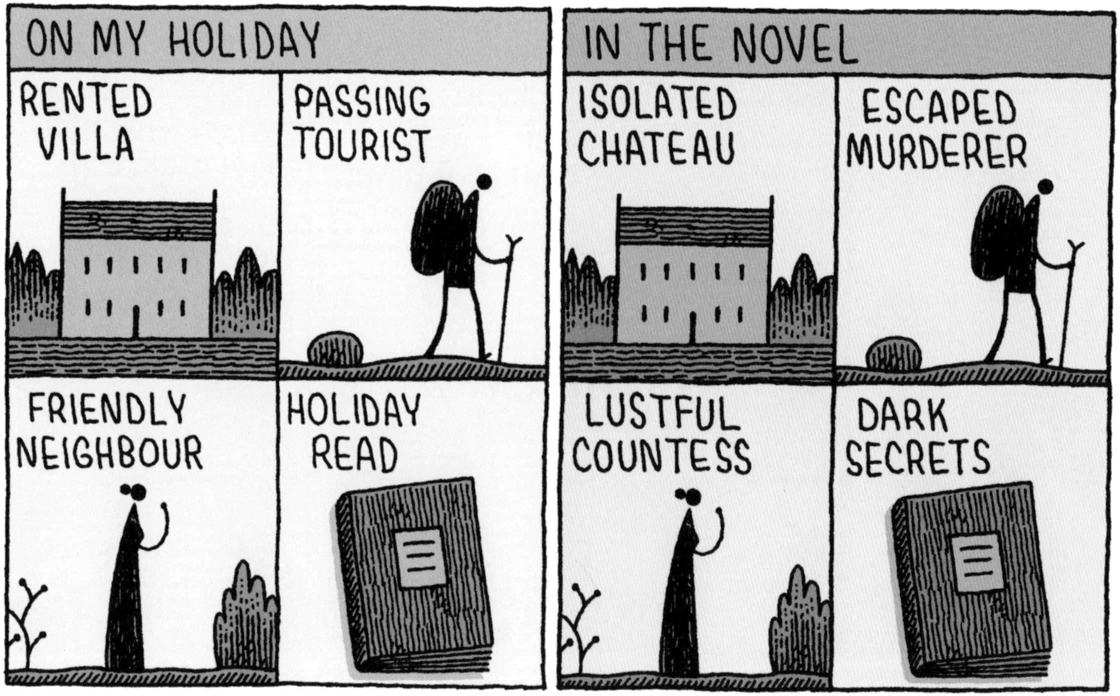

ON MY HOLIDAY
RENTED VILLA
PASSING TOURIST
FRIENDLY NEIGHBOUR
HOLIDAY READ
IN THE NOVEL
ISOLATED CHATEAU
ESCAPED MURDERER
LUSTFUL COUNTESS
DARK SECRETS

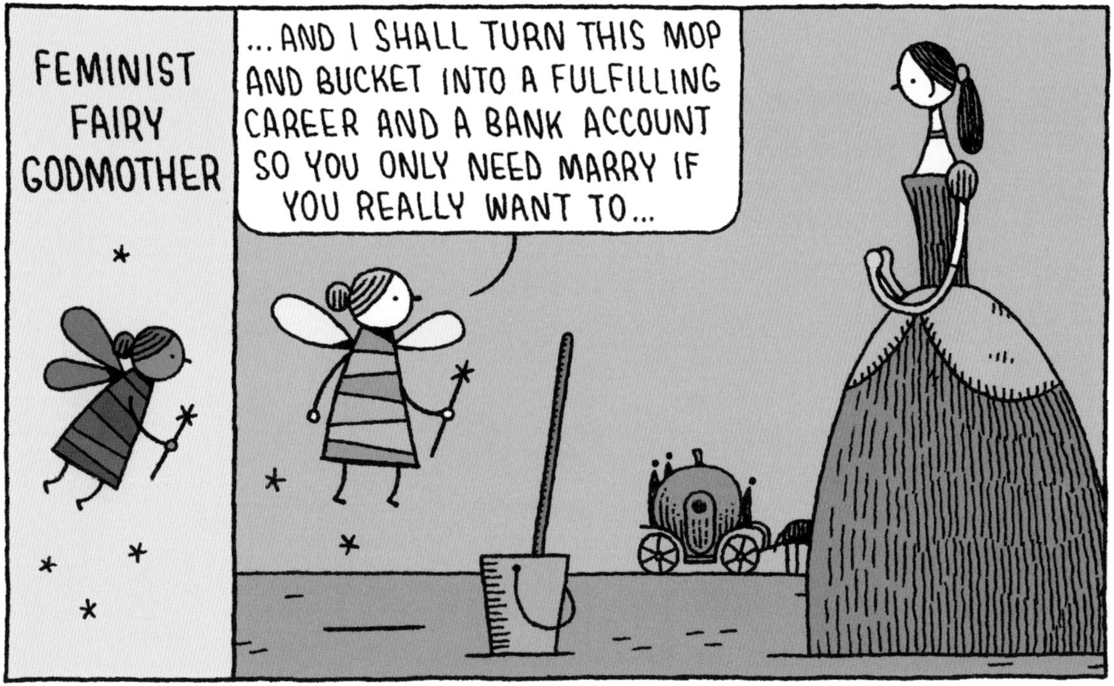
FEMINIST FAIRY GODMOTHER
...AND I SHALL TURN THIS MOP AND BUCKET INTO A FULFILLING CAREER AND A BANK ACCOUNT SO YOU ONLY NEED MARRY IF YOU REALLY WANT TO...

AGAINST WHOM HAVE YOU SWORN VENGEANCE?

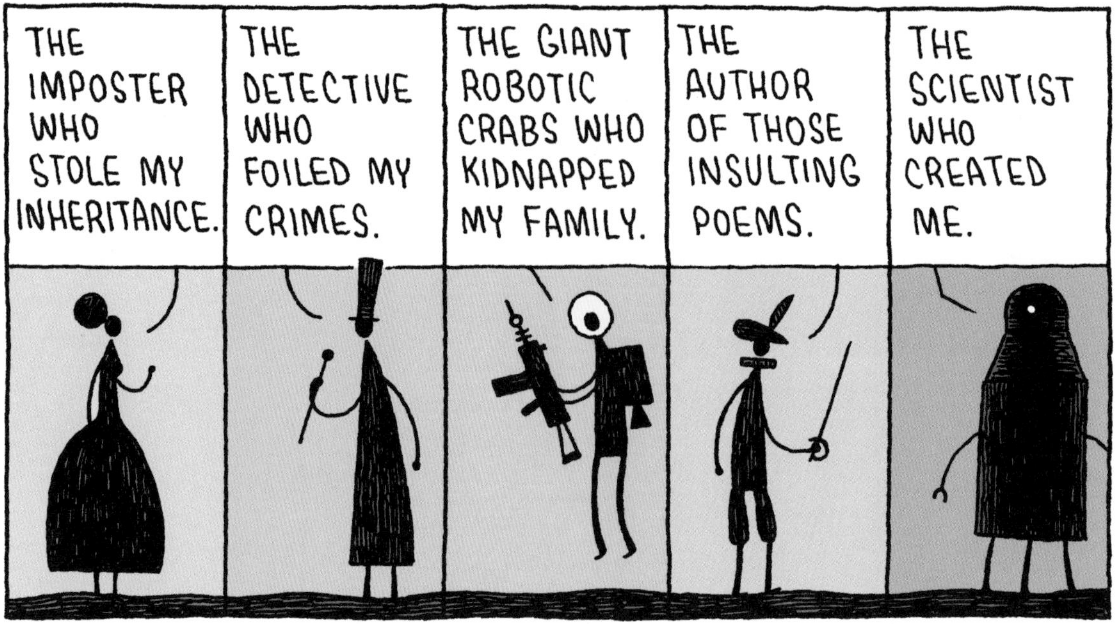

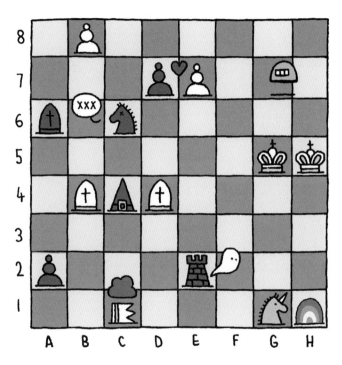

1. ILLICIT LOVE: D7, E7
2. WITCH TRIAL: C4
3. DRUNKEN KNIGHT INSULTS BISHOP: C6
4. UFO: G7
5. HAUNTING: F2
6. EXISTENTIAL DESPAIR: C1
7. LONG-LOST TWIN: G5
8. HAPPY ENDING: H1

QUEEN VICTORIA, CAMOUFLAGED BY HER MOURNING CLOTHES,
AVOIDS ABDUCTION BY THE ALIENS.
HER BRIGHTLY-ATTIRED COMPANION IS NOT SO LUCKY.

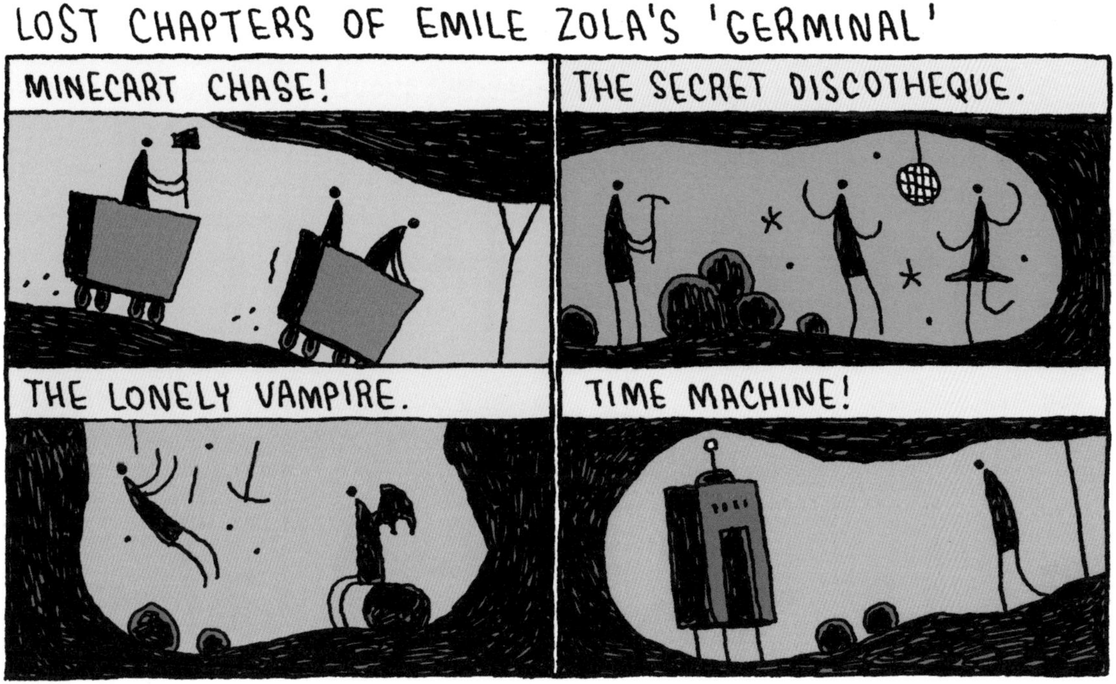
LOST CHAPTERS OF EMILE ZOLA'S 'GERMINAL'
MINECART CHASE!
THE SECRET DISCOTHEQUE.
THE LONELY VAMPIRE.
TIME MACHINE!

VARIOUS SCENES INVOLVING PUDDING

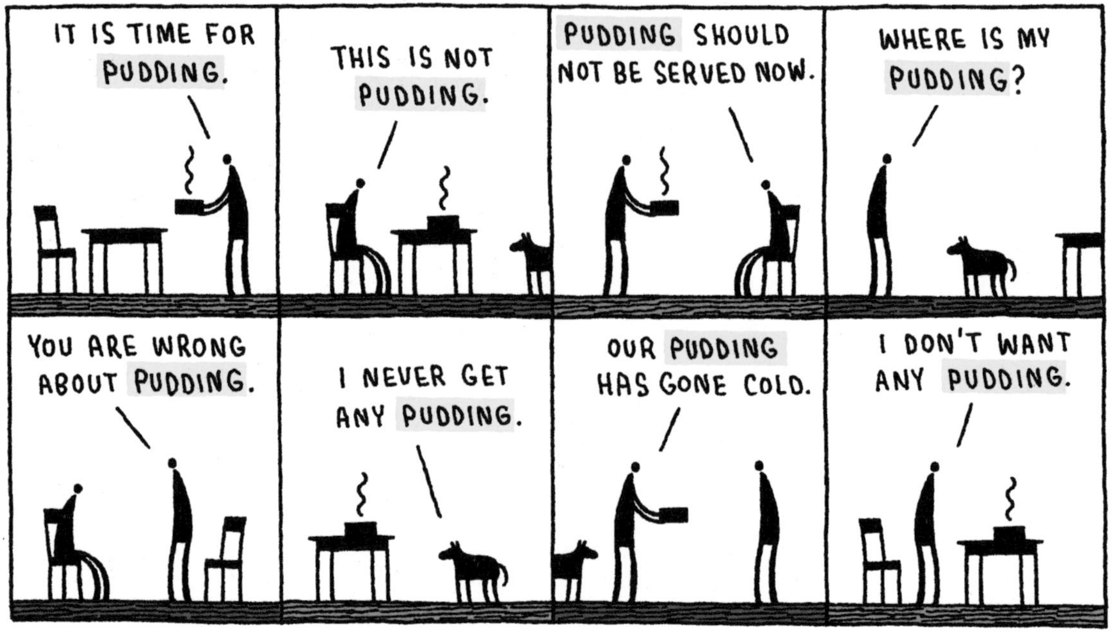
IT IS TIME FOR PUDDING.
THIS IS NOT PUDDING.
PUDDING SHOULD NOT BE SERVED NOW.
WHERE IS MY PUDDING?
YOU ARE WRONG ABOUT PUDDING.
I NEVER GET ANY PUDDING.
OUR PUDDING HAS GONE COLD.
I DON'T WANT ANY PUDDING.

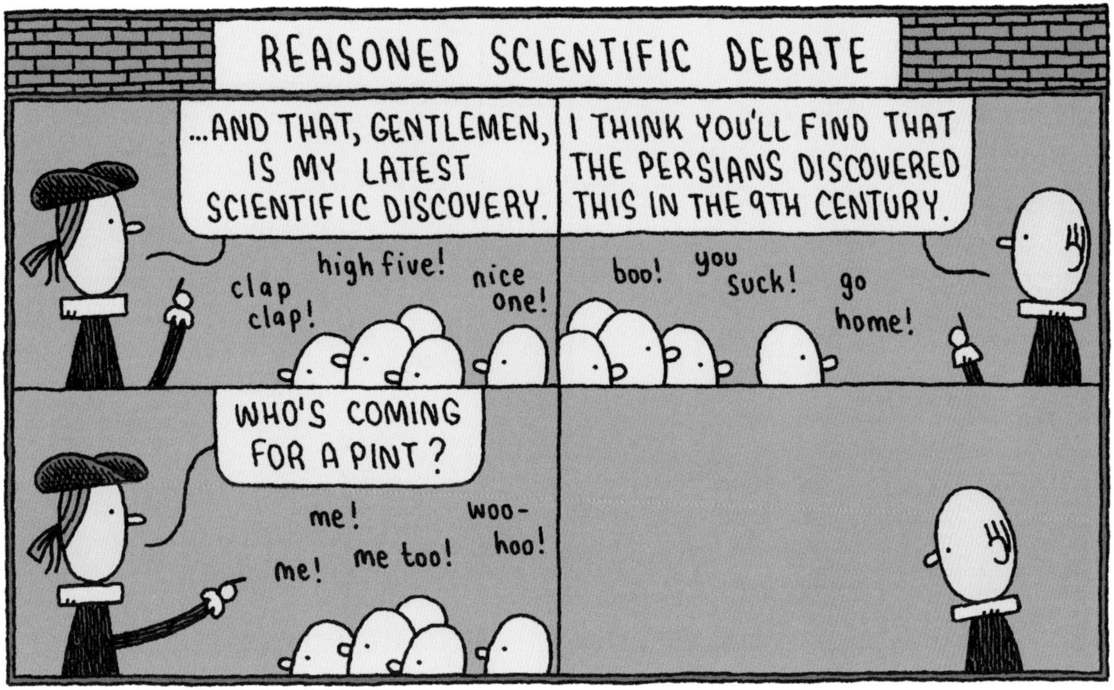
REASONED SCIENTIFIC DEBATE
...AND THAT, GENTLEMEN, IS MY LATEST SCIENTIFIC DISCOVERY.
clap clap!
high five!
nice one!
I THINK YOU'LL FIND THAT THE PERSIANS DISCOVERED THIS IN THE 9TH CENTURY.
boo!
you suck!
go home!
WHO'S COMING FOR A PINT?
me!
me!
me too!
woo-hoo!

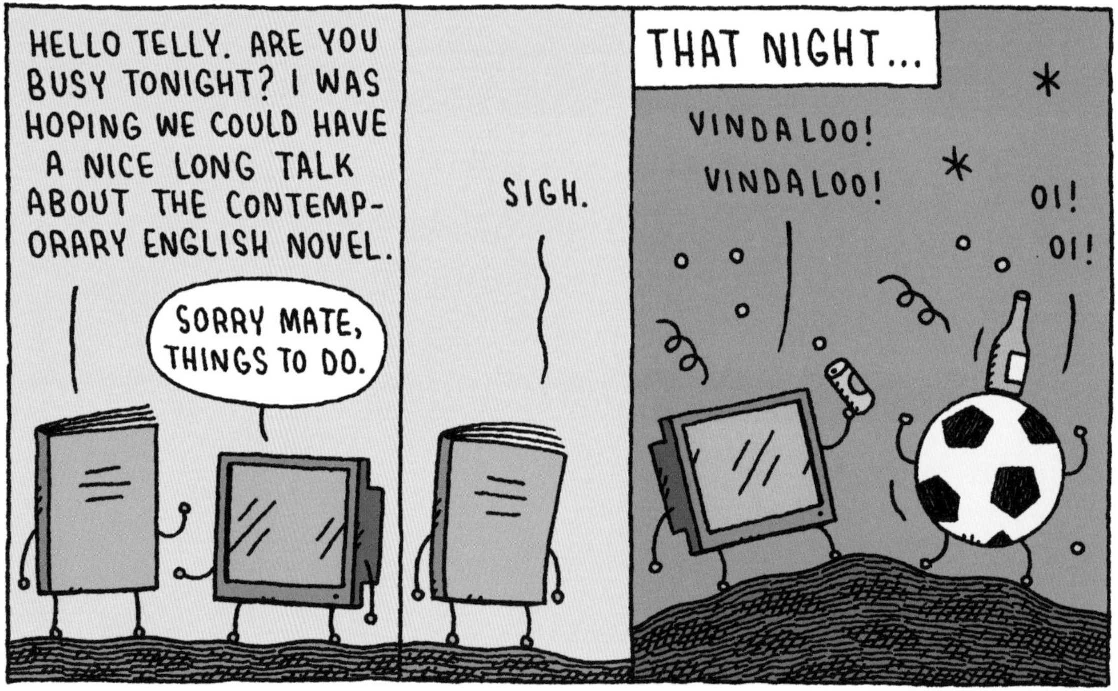
HELLO TELLY. ARE YOU BUSY TONIGHT? I WAS HOPING WE COULD HAVE A NICE LONG TALK ABOUT THE CONTEMPORARY ENGLISH NOVEL.
SORRY MATE, THINGS TO DO.
SIGH.
THAT NIGHT...
VINDALOO! VINDALOO!
OI! OI!

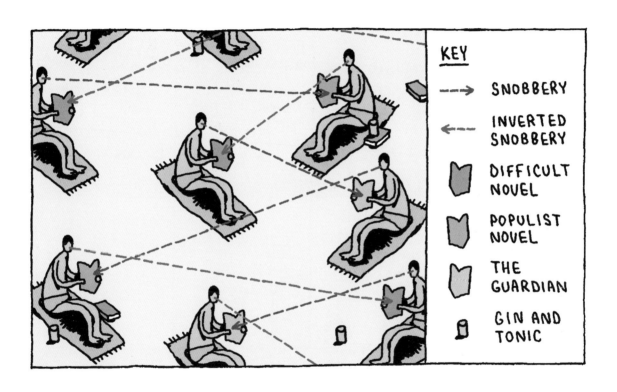

KEY

- - - → SNOBBERY
← - - - INVERTED SNOBBERY
DIFFICULT NOVEL
POPULIST NOVEL
THE GUARDIAN
GIN AND TONIC

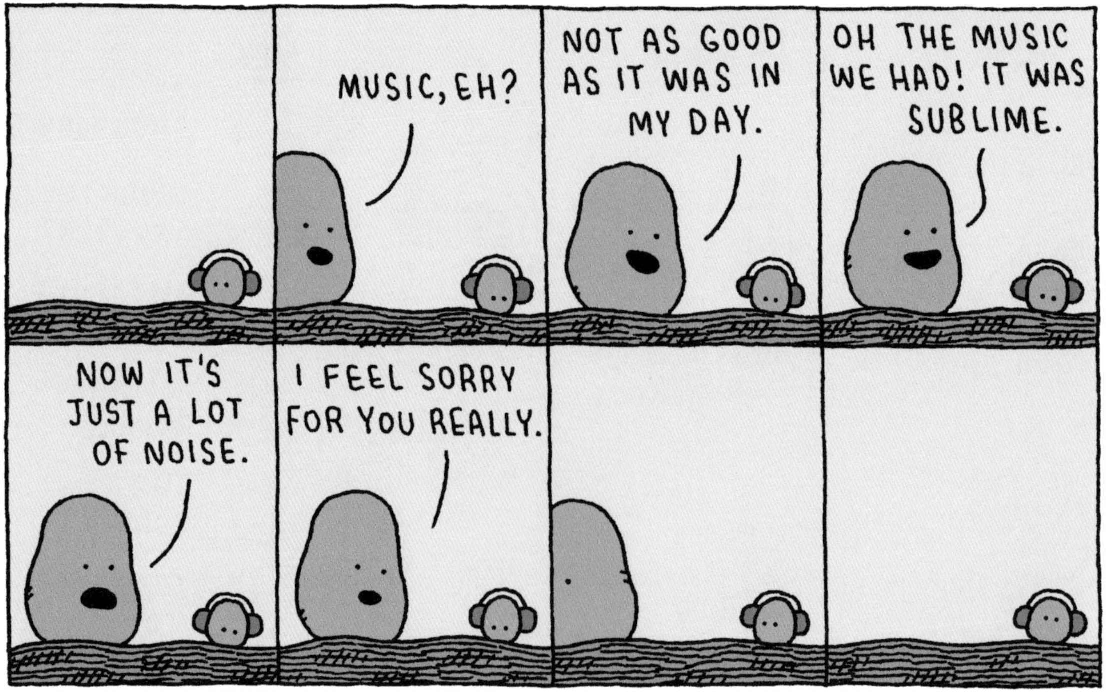
MUSIC, EH?
NOT AS GOOD AS IT WAS IN MY DAY.
OH THE MUSIC WE HAD! IT WAS SUBLIME.
NOW IT'S JUST A LOT OF NOISE.
I FEEL SORRY FOR YOU REALLY.

OUR SEASON OF INNOVATIVE SHAKESPEARE PRODUCTIONS
FLEA MACBETH
ALL HAIL MACBETH!
KING LEAR ON ICE
ACTION HAMLET!
TODDLER CORIOLANUS
HENRY V DOWN A WELL
OH! YOU GODS!!
ROBOT PERICLES
SKYPE ROMEO AND JULIET

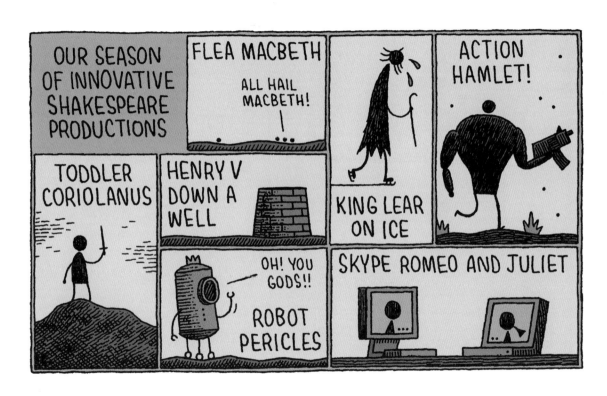

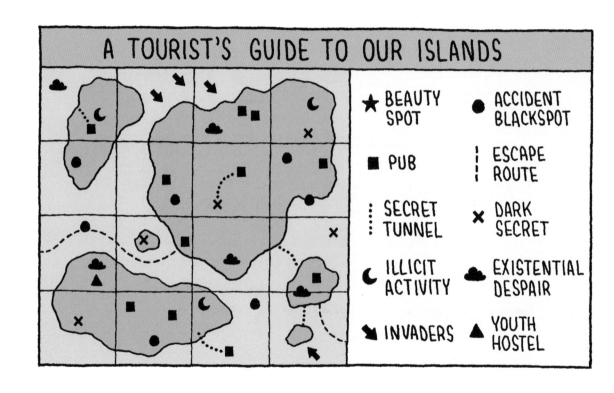

A TOURIST'S GUIDE TO OUR ISLANDS

★ BEAUTY SPOT

● ACCIDENT BLACKSPOT

■ PUB

⁝ ESCAPE ROUTE

⁝ SECRET TUNNEL

✕ DARK SECRET

☾ ILLICIT ACTIVITY

☁ EXISTENTIAL DESPAIR

➘ INVADERS

▲ YOUTH HOSTEL

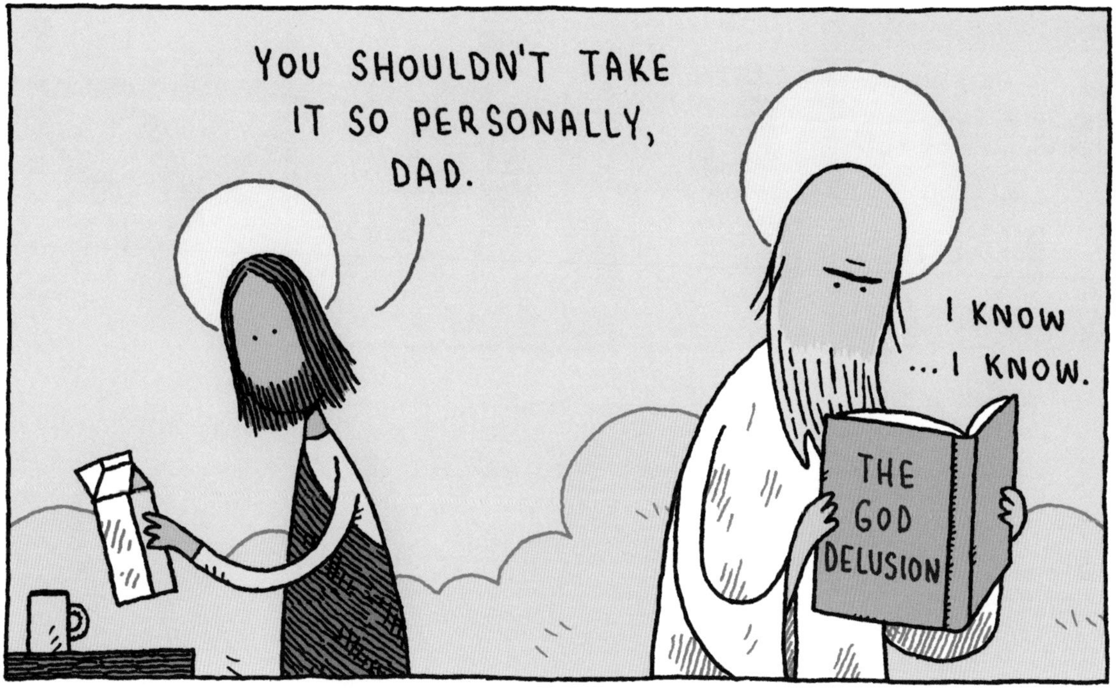
YOU SHOULDN'T TAKE IT SO PERSONALLY, DAD.
I KNOW ... I KNOW.
THE GOD DELUSION

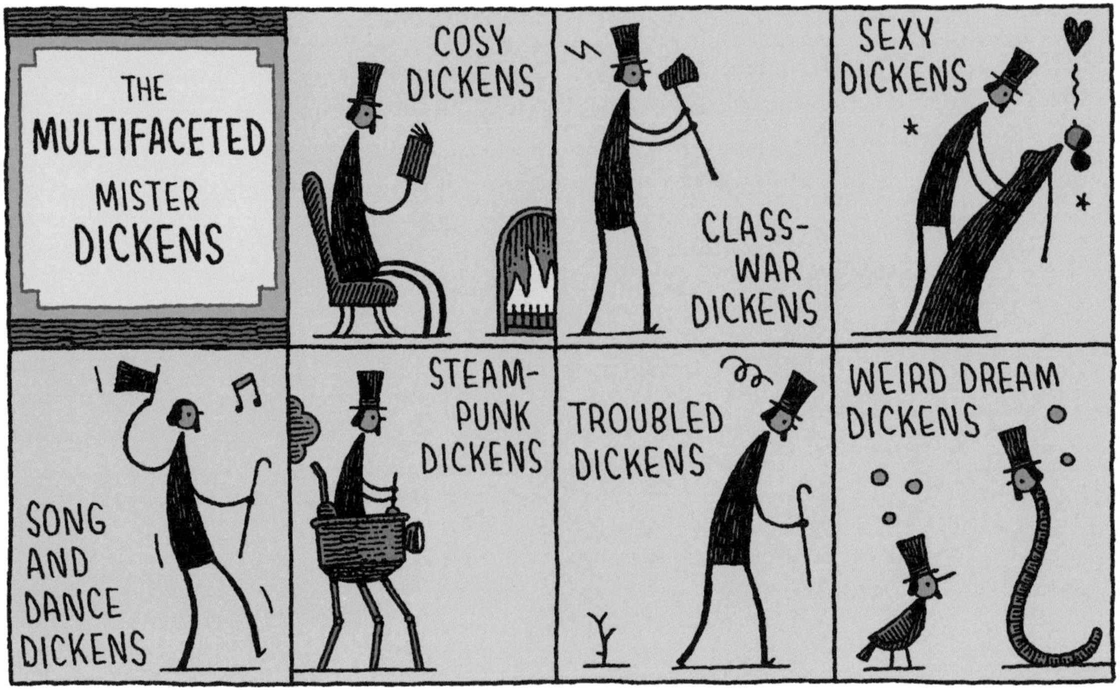

THE MULTIFACETED MISTER DICKENS
COSY DICKENS
CLASS-WAR DICKENS
SEXY DICKENS
SONG AND DANCE DICKENS
STEAM-PUNK DICKENS
TROUBLED DICKENS
WEIRD DREAM DICKENS

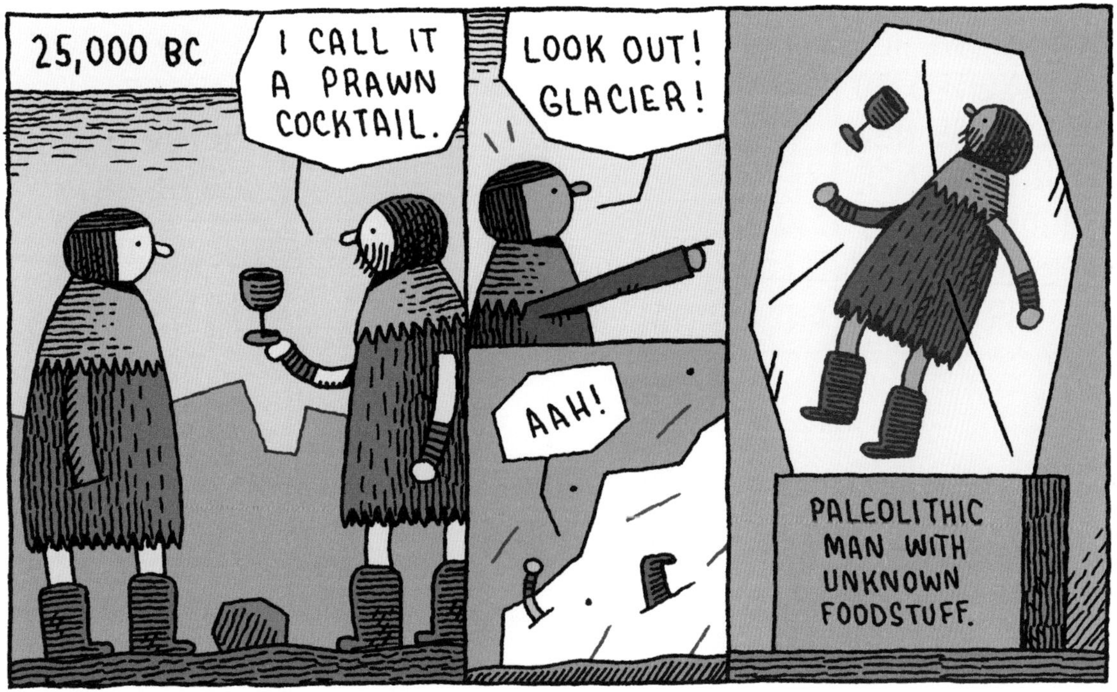
25,000 BC
I CALL IT A PRAWN COCKTAIL.
LOOK OUT! GLACIER!
AAH!
PALEOLITHIC MAN WITH UNKNOWN FOODSTUFF.

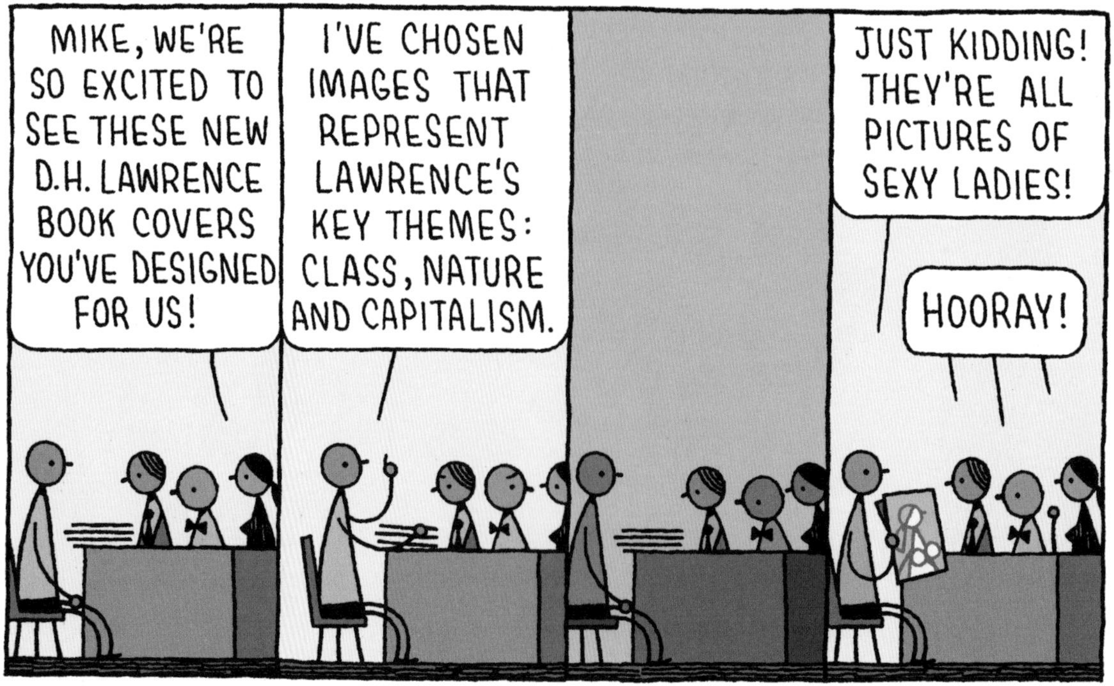
MIKE, WE'RE SO EXCITED TO SEE THESE NEW D.H. LAWRENCE BOOK COVERS YOU'VE DESIGNED FOR US!
I'VE CHOSEN IMAGES THAT REPRESENT LAWRENCE'S KEY THEMES: CLASS, NATURE AND CAPITALISM.
JUST KIDDING! THEY'RE ALL PICTURES OF SEXY LADIES!
HOORAY!

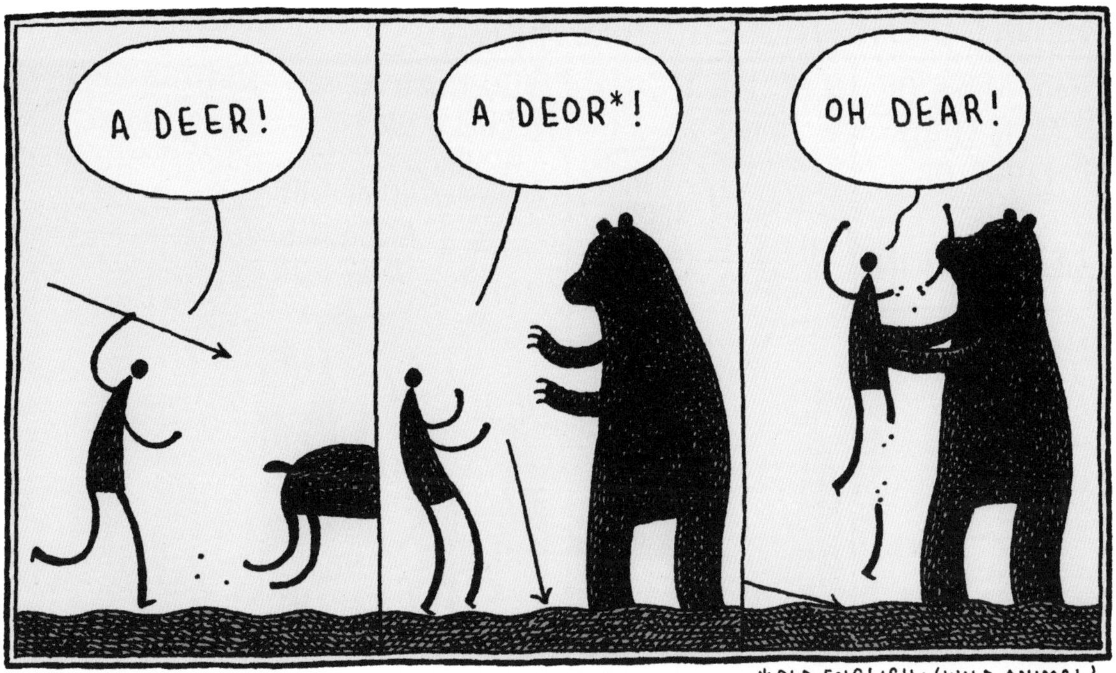
A DEER!
A DEOR*!
OH DEAR!

*OLD ENGLISH: 'WILD ANIMAL.'

HENRY DAVID THOREAU AND FRIENDS

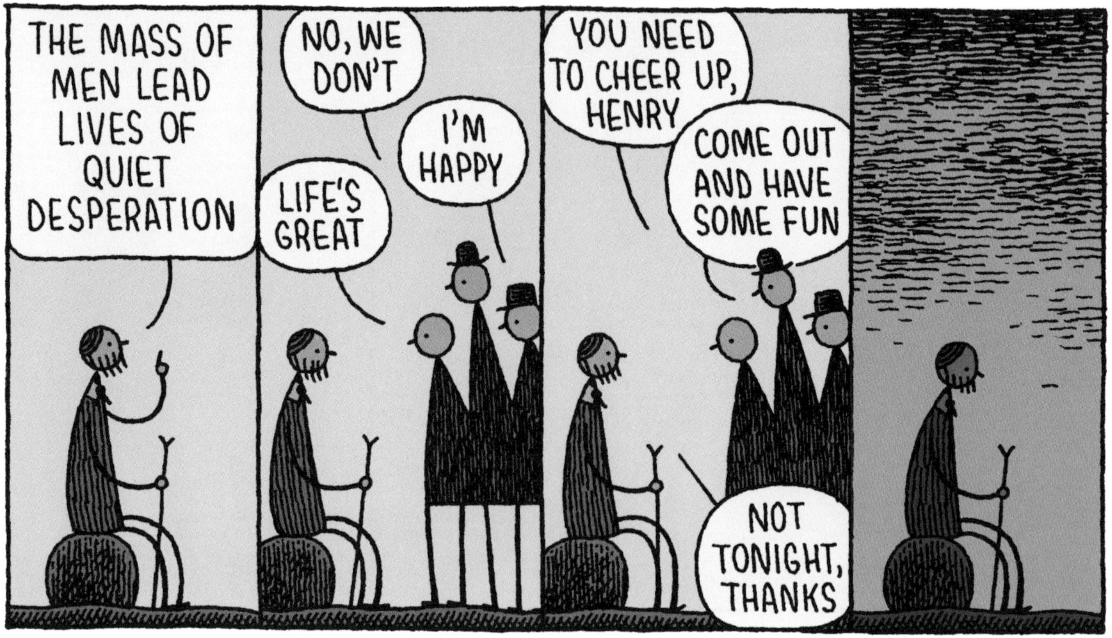

THE MASS OF MEN LEAD LIVES OF QUIET DESPERATION
NO, WE DON'T
LIFE'S GREAT
I'M HAPPY
YOU NEED TO CHEER UP, HENRY
COME OUT AND HAVE SOME FUN
NOT TONIGHT, THANKS

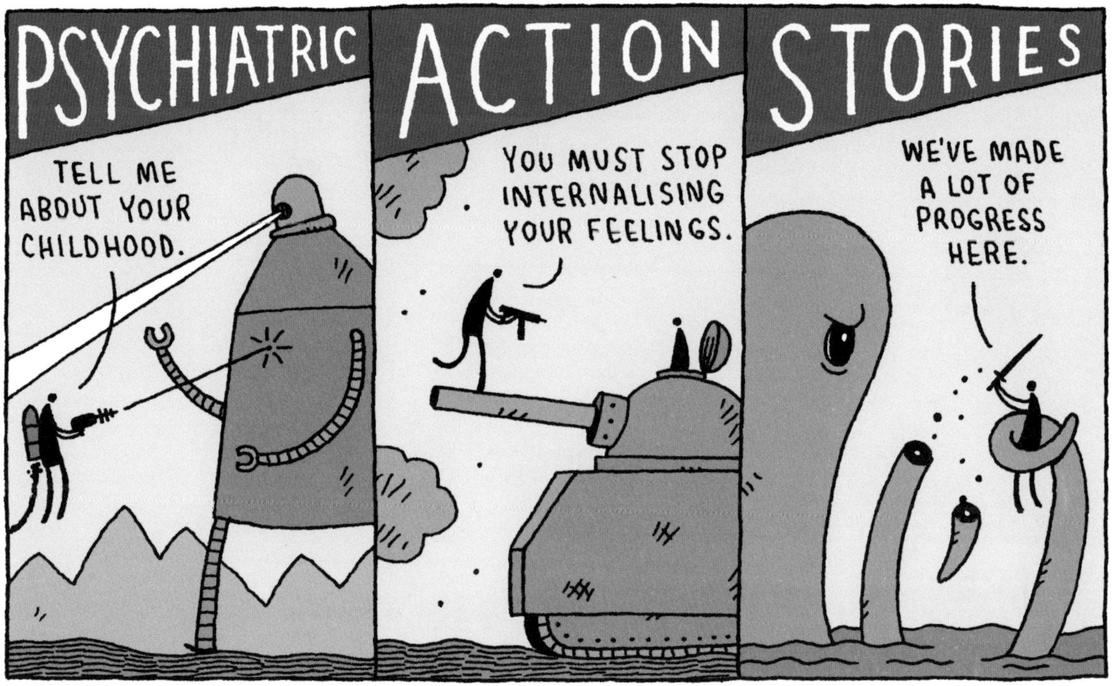
PSYCHIATRIC
TELL ME ABOUT YOUR CHILDHOOD.
ACTION
YOU MUST STOP INTERNALISING YOUR FEELINGS.
STORIES
WE'VE MADE A LOT OF PROGRESS HERE.

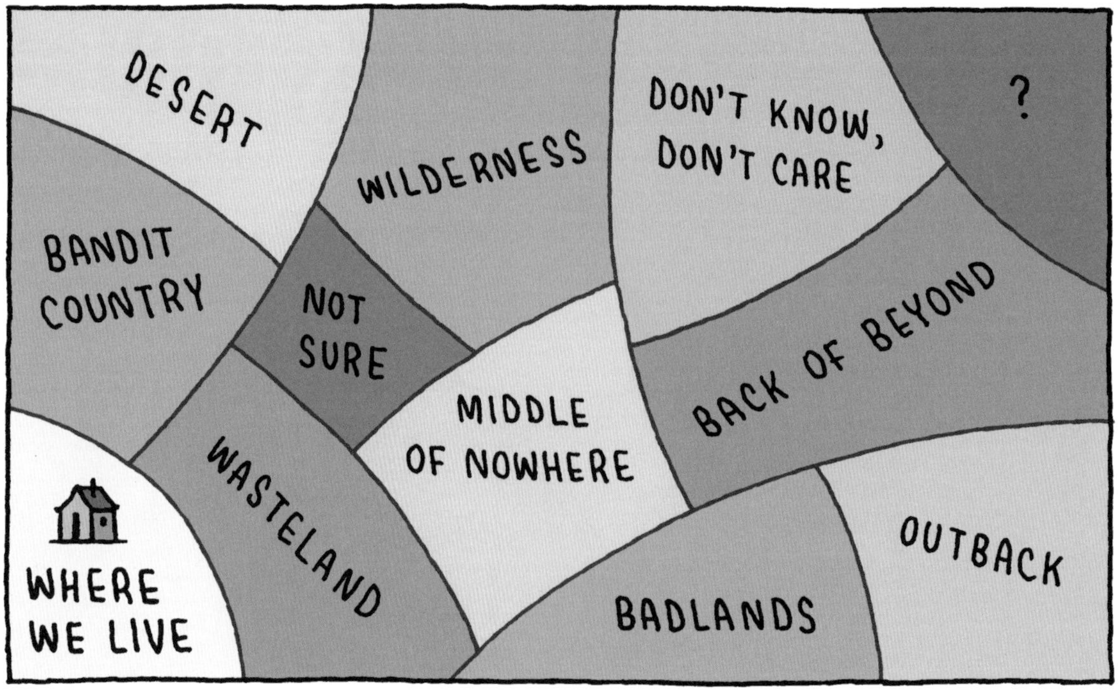
DESERT
WILDERNESS
DON'T KNOW, DON'T CARE
?
BANDIT COUNTRY
NOT SURE
MIDDLE OF NOWHERE
BACK OF BEYOND
WASTELAND
WHERE WE LIVE
BADLANDS
OUTBACK

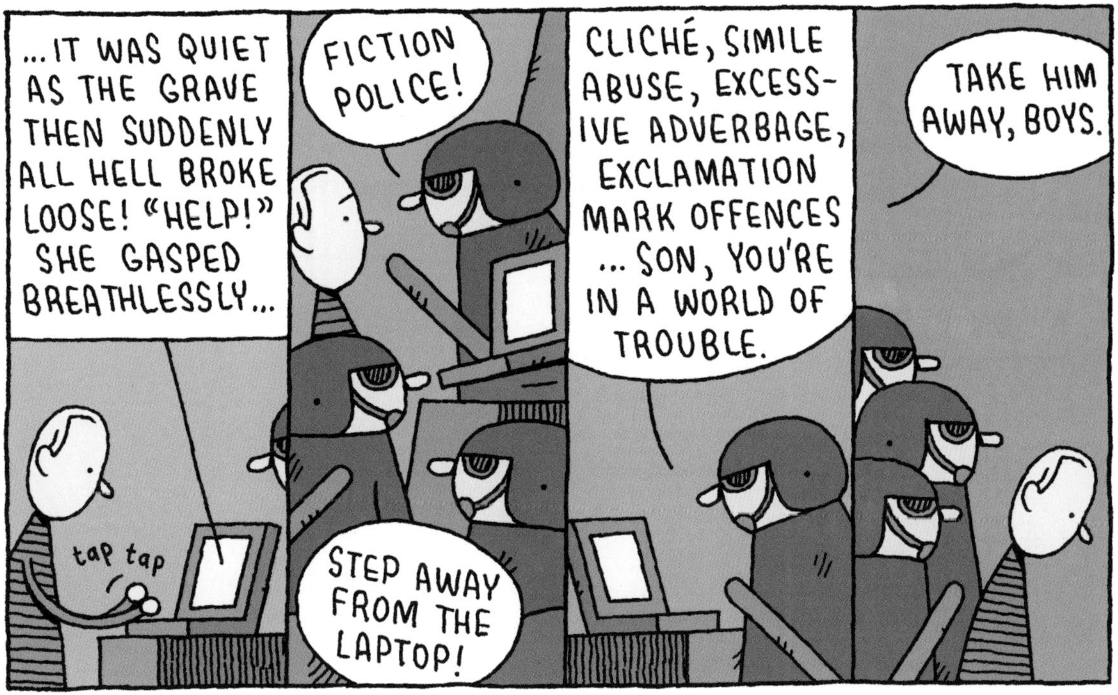
...IT WAS QUIET AS THE GRAVE THEN SUDDENLY ALL HELL BROKE LOOSE! "HELP!" SHE GASPED BREATHLESSLY...
tap tap
FICTION POLICE!
STEP AWAY FROM THE LAPTOP!
CLICHÉ, SIMILE ABUSE, EXCESS-IVE ADVERBAGE, EXCLAMATION MARK OFFENCES ...SON, YOU'RE IN A WORLD OF TROUBLE.
TAKE HIM AWAY, BOYS.

MECHANICAL SPACE-HORSE

EVERYONE THINKS YOU'RE JUST A PILE OF OLD JUNK, BUT I KNOW WE CAN WIN THE MOON DERBY!
1ST
MOON NEWS
ROBOT HORSE WINS DERBY
I LOVE YOU, MECHANICAL SPACE-HORSE!

BASEBALL EXPLAINED

US
THEM
GOOD INTENTIONS
9TH AND HENNEPIN
COMMUNITY CHEST
BROKEN DREAMS
GRASSY KNOLL
THE FARMER WANTS A WIFE
FOOD COURT
NO TRUMPS
OTHER

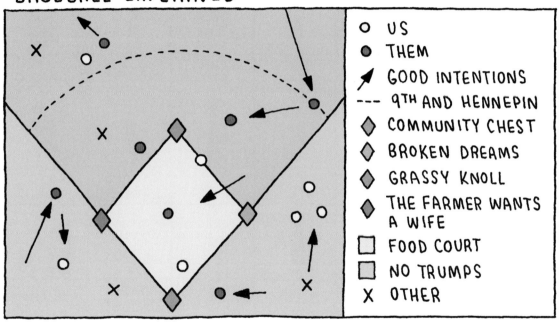

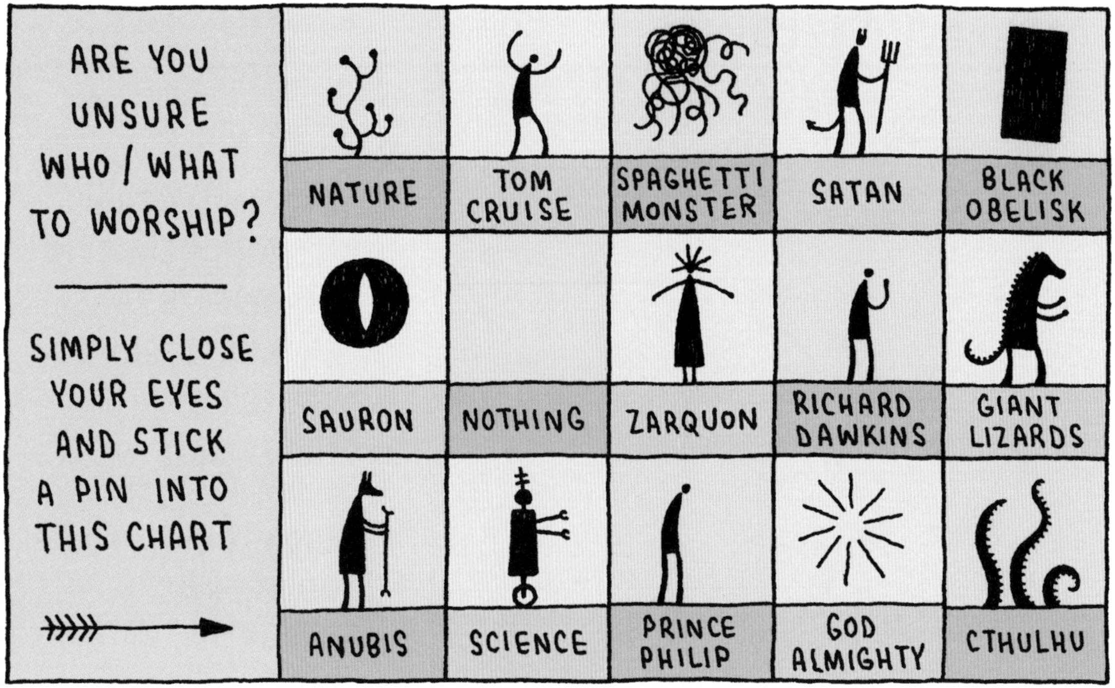
ARE YOU UNSURE WHO / WHAT TO WORSHIP?
SIMPLY CLOSE YOUR EYES AND STICK A PIN INTO THIS CHART
NATURE
TOM CRUISE
SPAGHETTI MONSTER
SATAN
BLACK OBELISK
SAURON
NOTHING
ZARQUON
RICHARD DAWKINS
GIANT LIZARDS
ANUBIS
SCIENCE
PRINCE PHILIP
GOD ALMIGHTY
CTHULHU

A PENGUIN'S VIEWS ON MODERN ARCHITECTURE

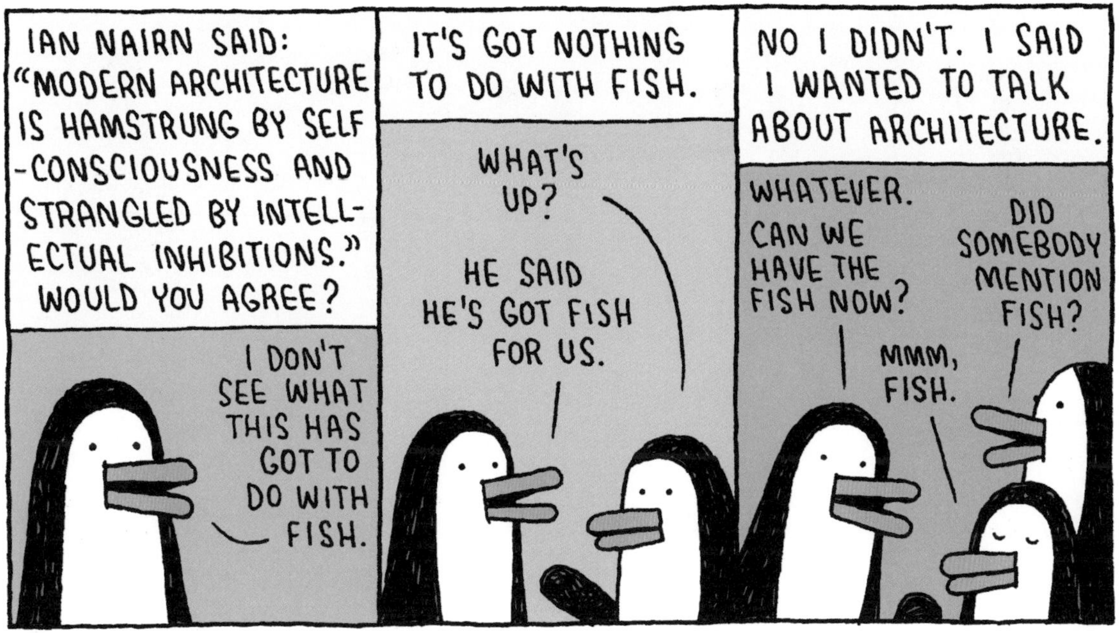

IAN NAIRN SAID: "MODERN ARCHITECTURE IS HAMSTRUNG BY SELF-CONSCIOUSNESS AND STRANGLED BY INTELLECTUAL INHIBITIONS." WOULD YOU AGREE?
I DON'T SEE WHAT THIS HAS GOT TO DO WITH FISH.
IT'S GOT NOTHING TO DO WITH FISH.
WHAT'S UP?
HE SAID HE'S GOT FISH FOR US.
NO I DIDN'T. I SAID I WANTED TO TALK ABOUT ARCHITECTURE.
WHATEVER.
CAN WE HAVE THE FISH NOW?
MMM, FISH.
DID SOMEBODY MENTION FISH?

A MONUMENT TO A GREAT MAN

| ERECTED | IGNORED | CAMPAIGNED AGAINST | REMOVED | REPLACED |

ATTITUDES TOWARD SEX IN THE MIDDLE AGES

fig. 1: Geoffrey Chaucer, c1370

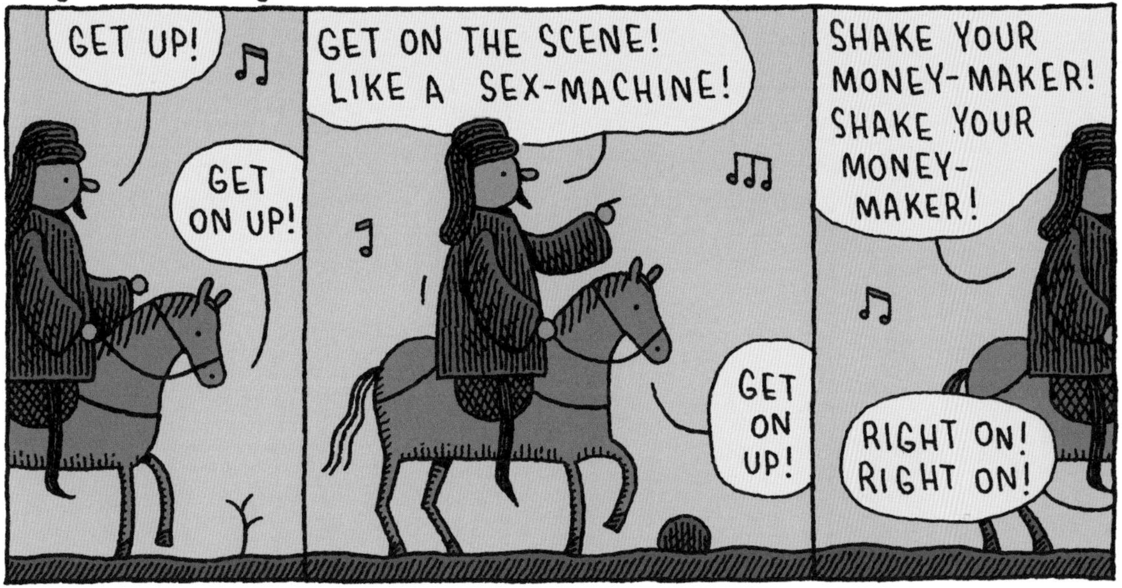
GET UP!
GET ON UP!
GET ON THE SCENE! LIKE A SEX-MACHINE!
GET ON UP!
SHAKE YOUR MONEY-MAKER! SHAKE YOUR MONEY-MAKER!
RIGHT ON! RIGHT ON!

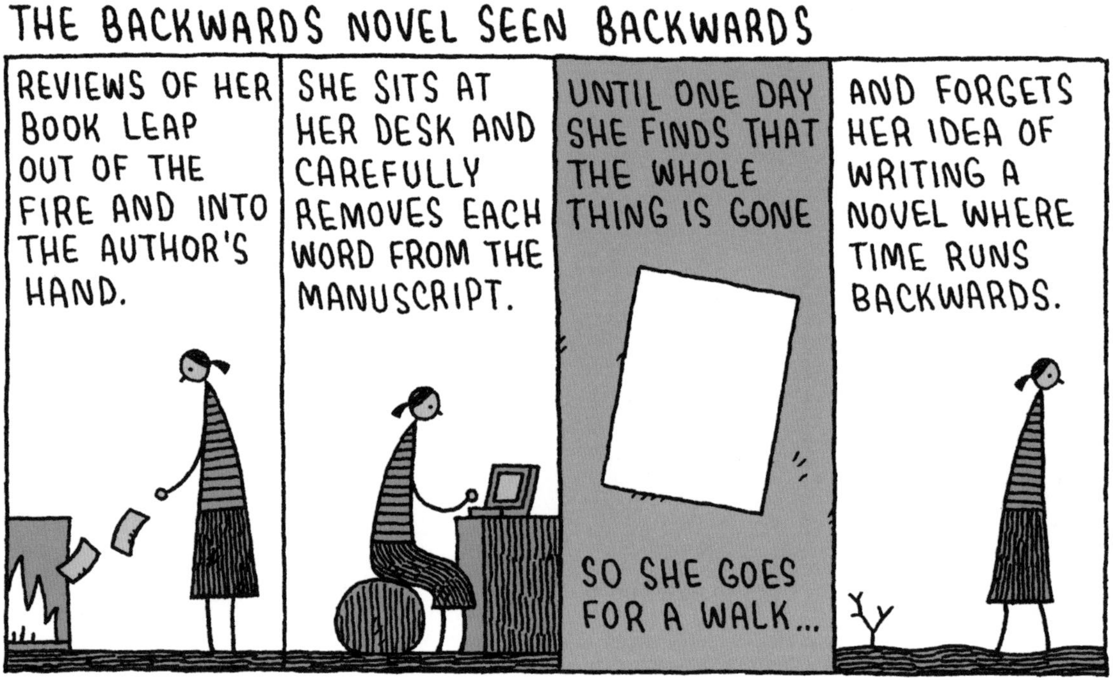
THE BACKWARDS NOVEL SEEN BACKWARDS
REVIEWS OF HER BOOK LEAP OUT OF THE FIRE AND INTO THE AUTHOR'S HAND.
SHE SITS AT HER DESK AND CAREFULLY REMOVES EACH WORD FROM THE MANUSCRIPT.
UNTIL ONE DAY SHE FINDS THAT THE WHOLE THING IS GONE
SO SHE GOES FOR A WALK...
AND FORGETS HER IDEA OF WRITING A NOVEL WHERE TIME RUNS BACKWARDS.

THE SURREALIST ARCHITECT CONSIDERS IT HIS MASTERPIECE, BUT THE ESTATE AGENT IS HAVING TROUBLE FINDING A BUYER

1. LIVING ROOM 2. MASTER BEDROOM 3. BATHROOM 4. MOUTH-PORTAL 5. CHILDHOOD TERROR 6. INSECT CONVENT 7. FUNDAMENTAL EGG 8. ABBATOIR/CARNIVAL/WOMB 9. GUEST BEDROOM.

THE MODERN POET IS ASSISTED WITH ROYAL COMMISSIONS BY THE LOR-E-8 AUTOMATIC POEM GENERATOR

OCCASION
WEDDING
CORONATION
FUNERAL
TERRIBLE GAFFE
DENTAL WORK
WIN AT THE HORSES
TYPE
ODE
SONNET
HAIKU
LIMERICK
RIDDLE
FREE VERSE
DRINKING SONG
TONE
CELEBRATORY
WISTFUL
AMUSING YET RESPECTFUL
BAWDY
VAGUE
MAWKISH
GENERATE

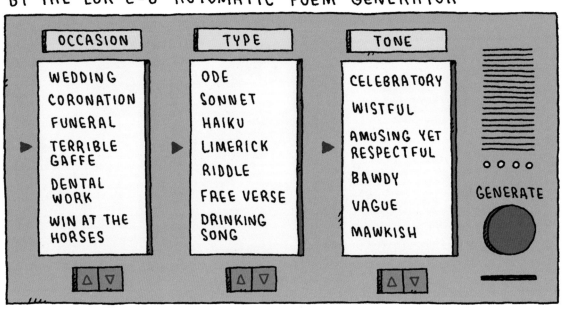

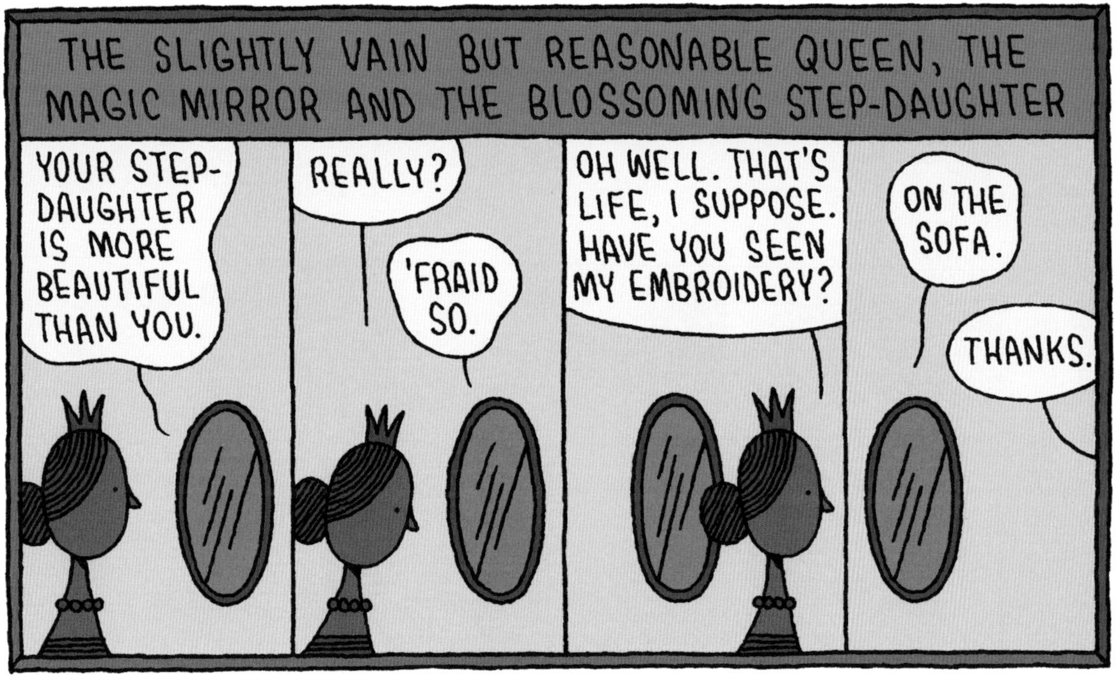
THE SLIGHTLY VAIN BUT REASONABLE QUEEN, THE MAGIC MIRROR AND THE BLOSSOMING STEP-DAUGHTER
YOUR STEP-DAUGHTER IS MORE BEAUTIFUL THAN YOU.
REALLY?
'FRAID SO.
OH WELL. THAT'S LIFE, I SUPPOSE. HAVE YOU SEEN MY EMBROIDERY?
ON THE SOFA.
THANKS.

THE PAPERS OF A GREAT WRITER
ILLEGIBLE SCRIBBLES
UNPRINTABLE FILTH
DOODLES
SUBLIME GENIUS
OBSCURE RAMBLINGS
OTHER

SOME OF MY FORTHCOMING MYSTERY NOVELS

EASILY-DISTRACTED COWBOY DETECTIVE

HE'S OBVIOUSLY BEEN KILLED BY — WOW! I'VE GOT SOCKS JUST LIKE THOSE.

OVERLY-DRAMATIC ASTRONAUT DETECTIVE

O HORROR, HORROR!! TONGUE NOR HEART CANNOT CONCEIVE NOR NAME THEE!!

CATTY UNICYCLING DETECTIVE

I DON'T KNOW WHO KILLED YOUR HUSBAND BUT YOU HAVE WAYYY TOO MUCH MAKE-UP ON.

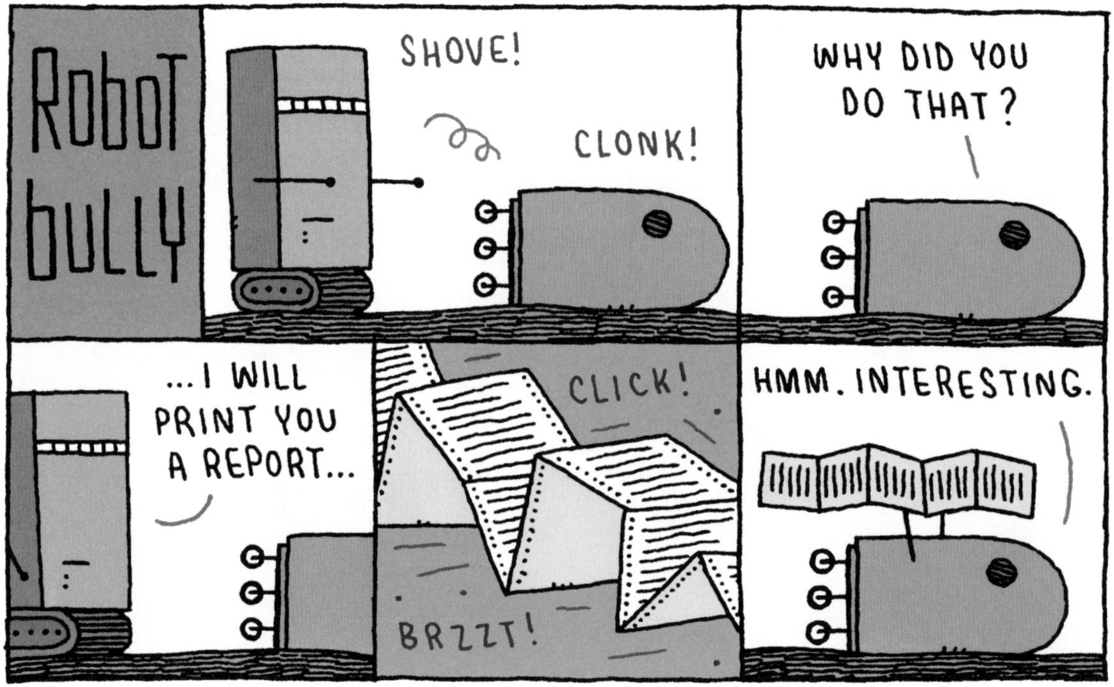
ROBOT BULLY
SHOVE!
CLONK!
WHY DID YOU DO THAT?
...I WILL PRINT YOU A REPORT...
CLICK!
BRZZT!
HMM. INTERESTING.

FOUR OBSTACLES TO WRITING

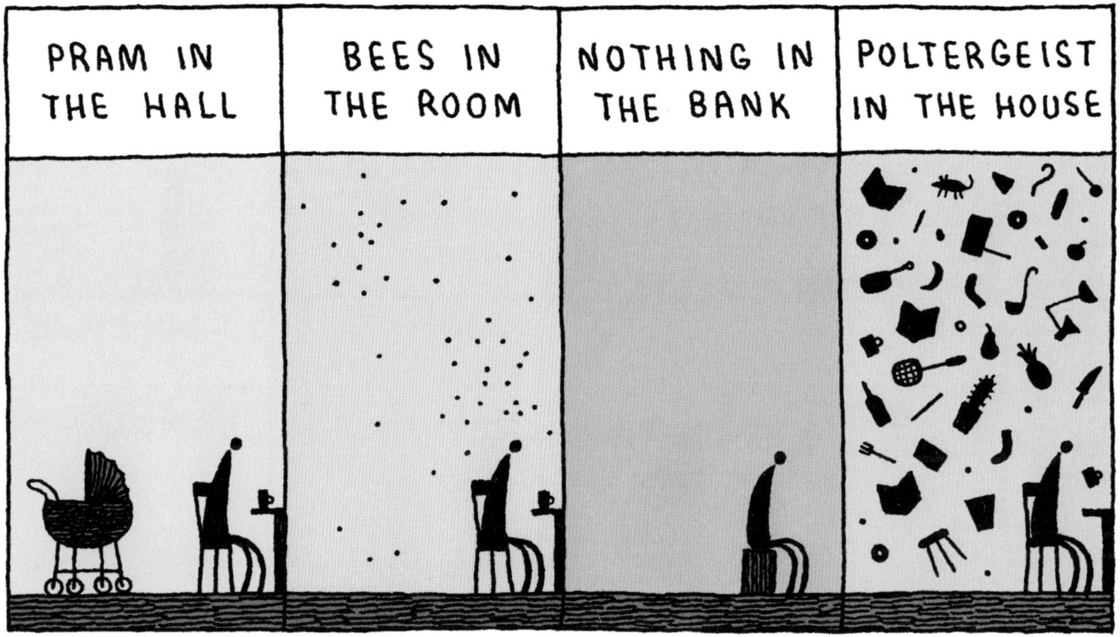
PRAM IN THE HALL
BEES IN THE ROOM
NOTHING IN THE BANK
POLTERGEIST IN THE HOUSE

CUT THIS OUT AND CARRY WITH YOU AT ALL TIMES.
IN THE EVENT OF MY DEATH I WOULD LIKE TO BE MEMORIALISED WITH (TICK ONE BOX):
SMALL PLAQUE
HEROIC STATUE
SPOOKY TREE
COLLOSAL ZIGGURAT
HAUNTED FRUIT MACHINE
NETWORK OF SECRET TUNNELS

3-D FRIENDS
HELLO! I'M A SPHERE.
...AND I'M A CUBE!
WE CAN NEVER TRULY KNOW ANY-ONE. WE ARE ALONE IN A COLD, UNCARING UNIVERSE.

THE REASON I WAS LATE EXPLAINED IN A DIAGRAM
UNCONSCIOUS DESIRES
CHILDHOOD FEARS
WATCHING 'KATIE AND PETER'
TRAFFIC
STOPPED WATCH
DRAWING THIS DIAGRAM
NEW SHOES TOO TIGHT
REPRESSED ANGER

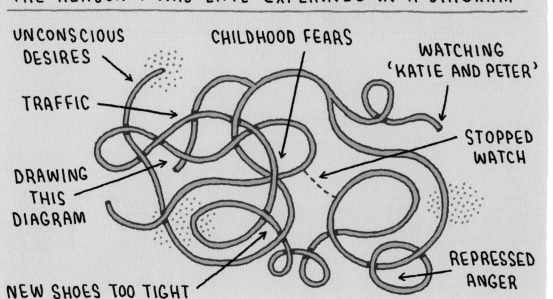

TELL ME A SCARY STORY GRAND-PÈRE.

OK.

NOT FAR FROM HERE LIES A DEEP, DARK FOREST. AND IN IT STANDS A CROOKED LITTLE HUT.

AND IN THAT HUT LIVES A STRANGE MAN. AND EVERY NIGHT HE SITS DOWN TO A BIG PLATE OF...

BRITISH FOOD!

AAH!

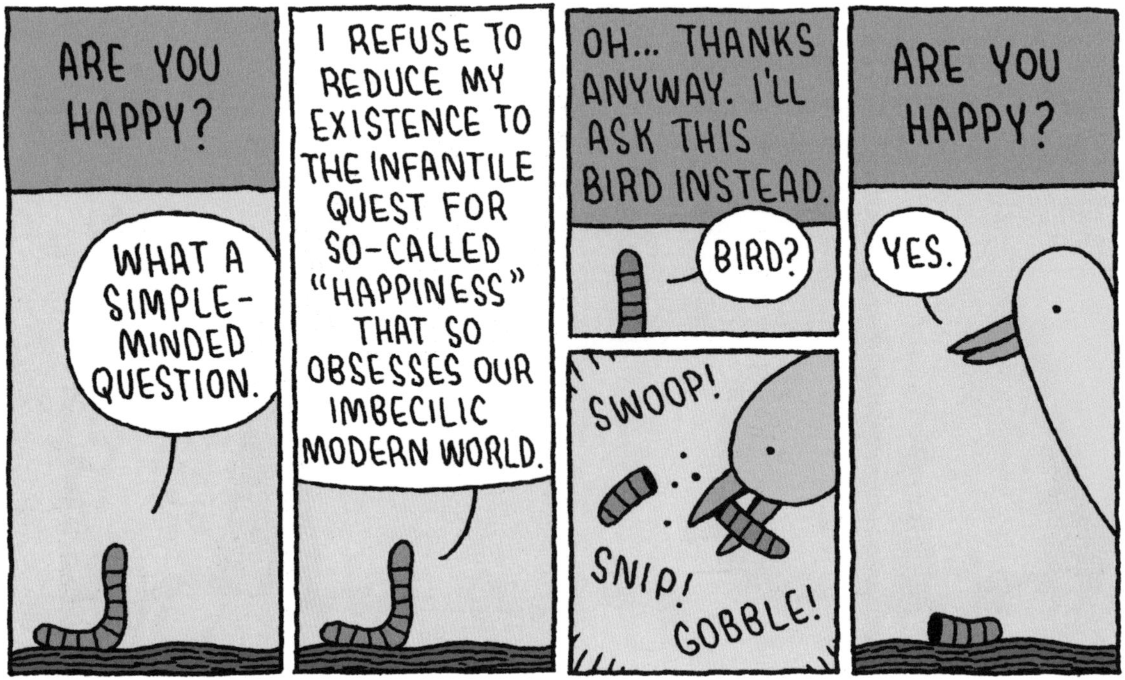
ARE YOU HAPPY?
WHAT A SIMPLE-MINDED QUESTION.
I REFUSE TO REDUCE MY EXISTENCE TO THE INFANTILE QUEST FOR SO-CALLED "HAPPINESS" THAT SO OBSESSES OUR IMBECILIC MODERN WORLD.
OH... THANKS ANYWAY. I'LL ASK THIS BIRD INSTEAD.
BIRD?
SWOOP!
SNIP!
GOBBLE!
ARE YOU HAPPY?
YES.

IN THE WINE CELLAR
KEY
○ FRUITY
■ OAKY
EASY DRINKING
X POISONED
* SPARKLING
▲ COMPLEX
● CURSED
? PROBABLY POISONED
! EXCEPTIONAL
HALLUCINOGENIC
▽ DESSERT WINE

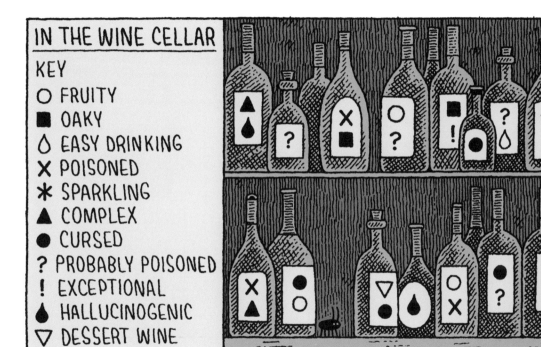

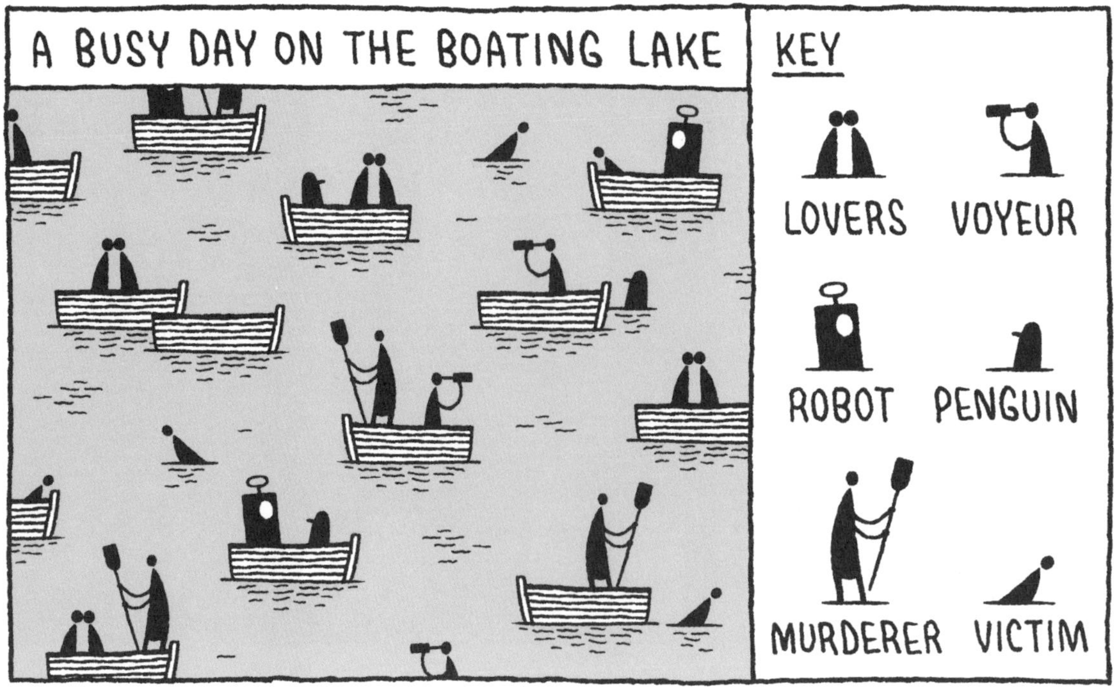
A BUSY DAY ON THE BOATING LAKE
KEY
LOVERS
VOYEUR
ROBOT
PENGUIN
MURDERER
VICTIM

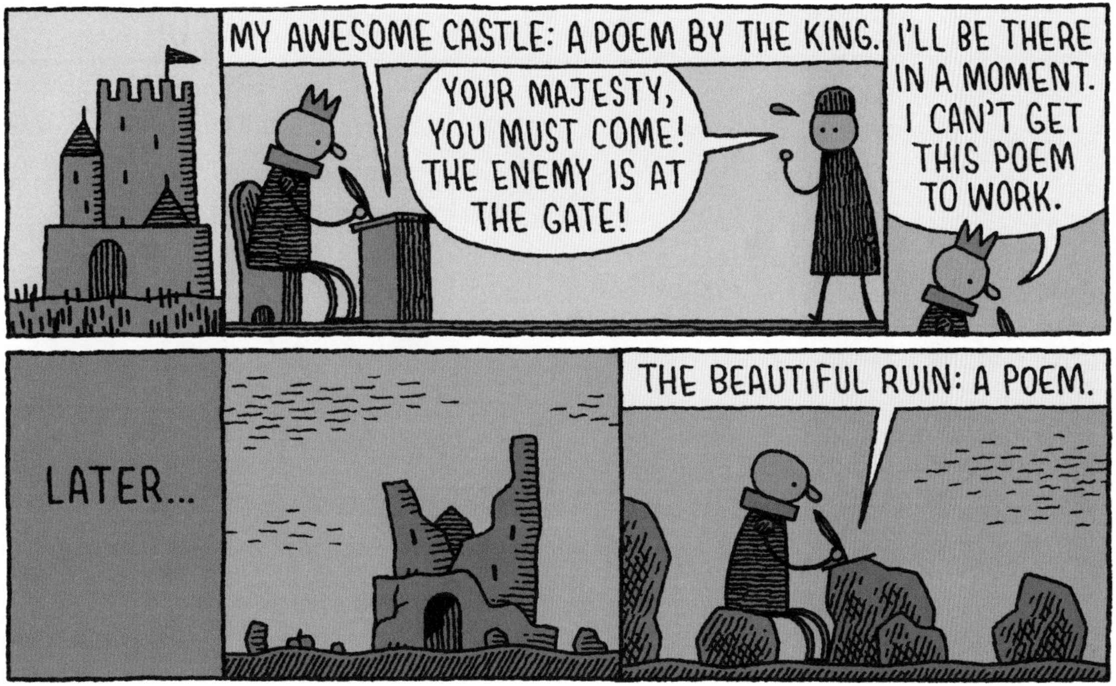
MY AWESOME CASTLE: A POEM BY THE KING.
YOUR MAJESTY, YOU MUST COME! THE ENEMY IS AT THE GATE!
I'LL BE THERE IN A MOMENT. I CAN'T GET THIS POEM TO WORK.
LATER...
THE BEAUTIFUL RUIN: A POEM.

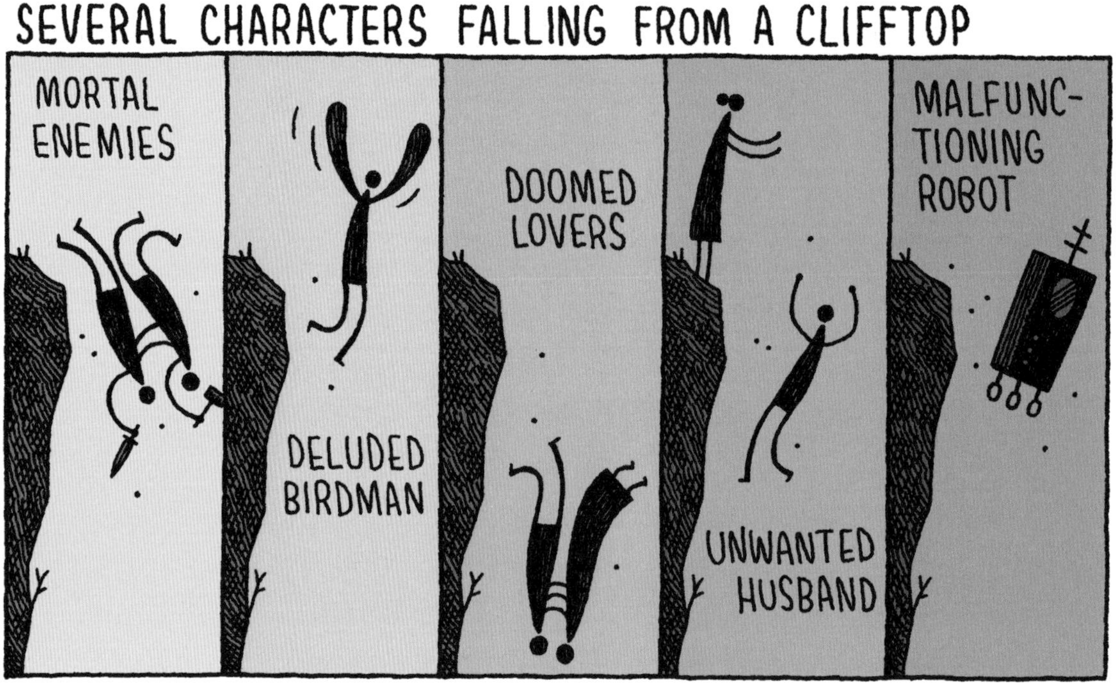
SEVERAL CHARACTERS FALLING FROM A CLIFFTOP
MORTAL ENEMIES
DELUDED BIRDMAN
DOOMED LOVERS
UNWANTED HUSBAND
MALFUNCTIONING ROBOT

THESE COMICS ORIGINALLY APPEARED IN THE GUARDIAN NEWSPAPER.
I WOULD LIKE TO THANK ROGER BROWNING, WHO COMMISSIONED
ME TO MAKE THEM FOR THE GUARDIAN AND WHO HAS ALWAYS
BEEN ENTHUSIASTIC AND DELIGHTFUL TO WORK WITH.
I WOULD ALSO LIKE TO THANK LISA ALLARDICE, PEGGY BURNS,
JESSICA CAMPBELL, TOM DEVLIN, MATTHEW FORSYTHE,
GINNY HOOKER, TRACY HURREN, BILLY KIOSOGLOU, CHRIS OLIVEROS,
JULIA POHL-MIRANDA, NICHOLAS WROE AND MY LOVELY WIFE, JO.

TOM GAULD WAS BORN IN 1976 AND GREW UP IN ABERDEENSHIRE,
SCOTLAND. HE STUDIED ILLUSTRATION AT EDINBURGH COLLEGE OF ART
AND THE ROYAL COLLEGE OF ART. HE WORKS AS A CARTOONIST AND
ILLUSTRATOR AND IS REGULARLY PUBLISHED IN THE GUARDIAN AND THE
NEW YORK TIMES. HIS GRAPHIC NOVEL 'GOLIATH' IS PUBLISHED BY
DRAWN AND QUARTERLY. HE LIVES IN LONDON WITH HIS FAMILY.

WWW.TOMGAULD.COM

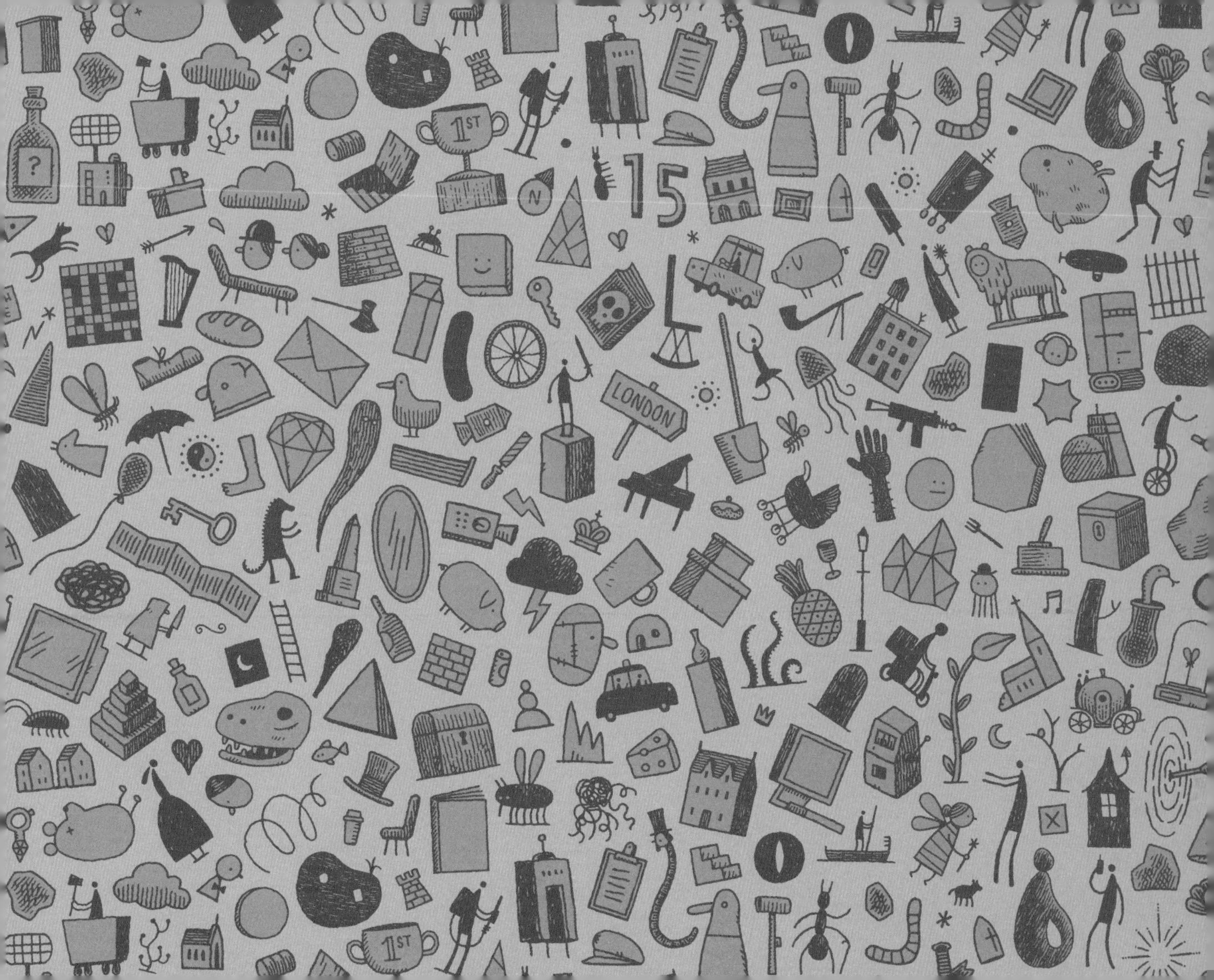
1ST
15
N
LONDON
?

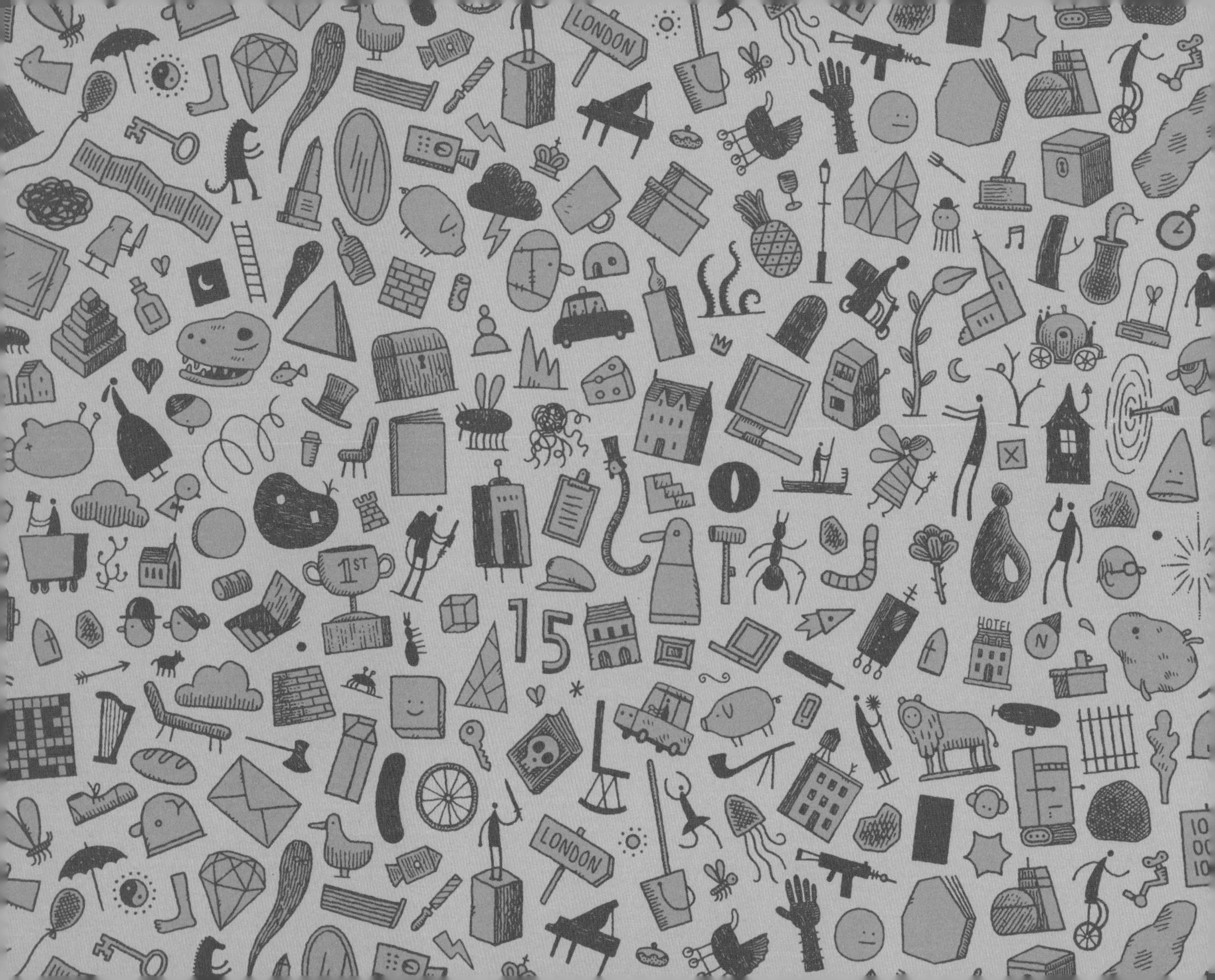
LONDON
1ST
15
HOTEL
N
LONDON